Table of Contents

Marketing and Market Research at a Glance

Industry Outlook

- **Consumer packaged goods companies** offer positions on a more consistent basis than other industry segments, though competition is stiff and burnout among brand managers and new product development managers is an issue. Market research expertise with new technology-assisted data collection techniques and experience with a high-profile global consumer branding company may give you the edge over the competition.

- **Professional service firms** are increasingly hiring marketers to bring a strategic customer orientation to a field that was previously sales-driven, although specialized knowledge of the field is often required. Expertise in CRM (customer relationship management) and reputation management is especially helpful.

- **Financial firms** have been scrambling to repair their reputations in the wake of revelations about alleged IPO kickbacks, insider trading, and a cooking of the books, and marketers with a grasp of law and finance may be just the ones to do it. The high rewards of this field come with substantial risks, namely market volatility and ethical quagmires.

- **Tech companies** are, in fact, still hiring—in particular, biotech, medical technology, and blue-chip firms that understand the need to express innovation in human terms for market success. Demonstrated business savvy plus a background in science or technology equals a winning combination for tech marketers.

- **Nonprofits** are paying more attention to marketing (which in the nonprofit field often falls into the general area of "fund development") to compete for a shrinking pool of government and foundation grants, private donations, and corporate sponsorships. Expertise in fee-for-service marketing and membership marketing are key qualifications in many of the larger, more stable organizations, and they are the most transferable skills for nonprofit marketers who want to keep their options open in the for-profit sector.

- **Across all industries**, market research is feeling the pinch of smaller research budgets, so researchers are shifting focus to low-cost, high-profit online surveys and other technology-assisted data collection methods and away from costly, time-intensive mail surveys and telephone research. Market researchers should triangulate their skill sets with a sound grasp of statistics and statistical software, qualitative methods such as focus groups and interviewing, and new media-assisted data collection techniques such as online surveying.

Opportunity Overview

- **Undergrads** prepared to tolerate number-crunching, intensive teamwork, and low starting pay for their first couple of years as marketing associates, brand assistants, or fund development assistants will find opportunities to find their market niche and pad their portfolios. Those with a solid grounding in statistics will have a better shot at entry-level market research analyst positions, which tend to pay more than other entry-level marketing positions.

- **MBAs** aid marketing career advancement at the executive level, but they don't hold as much sway as they once did and are no guarantee of signing bonuses. New MBAs should expect to enter low-level positions and advance gradually with a consistent track record of marketing wins. An MBA can help in landing a management position in market research, provided the course-work covered statistics and research methods. But keep in mind that PhDs in disciplines calling on strong communication and analytical skills—from statistics and math to psychology and politics—often have an edge over MBAs when it comes to snagging market research positions.

- **Midcareer professionals** may find business skills and industry know-how to be assets in establishing themselves in an industry-specific marketing niche, but they, too, will have to downshift to lower-level positions until they've got some solid wins behind them. Experience with statistical modeling software and research design could help midcareer candidates land market research positions. To attain a management position in market research, midcareer and other candi-dates will likely need at least a graduate degree in marketing, business, or statistics.

The Role

- Overview

- Hiring Trends

- Breakdown by Industry

- Trends in the Field

Overview

If you've ever watched a clever television ad and thought, "I could do that," be advised: There's far more to a marketer's job than meets the eye. What you don't see on television is all of the careful demographic and statistical analysis, extensive testing and surveys, supply and vendor management, and strategic thinking that goes into every word uttered on your television screen—a process that often takes specialized expertise and months of teamwork to complete. If your creative genius is matched by your analytical acumen, you may find that marketing makes for a worthy challenge, and an exciting career.

The uninitiated may mistakenly equate marketing with peddling household products, but marketers know their roles are far more complex and engaging than that. They help their organizations anticipate the public's needs and position them to satisfy those needs. As such, marketing is the necessary link between an organization and its target audience, which is now more broadly defined to include customers, clients, investors, and partners.

Where Research Comes In

If you often wonder why people behave the way they do, then you may be meant for a career in market research. Market researchers make it their business to uncover the strangest quirks of human behavior and apply their findings to identify social, economic, and political patterns. Market research runs the gamut from developing the methodology and metrics for a research project to crunching numbers, collecting data, and presenting your findings—which insiders say is much more exciting than it sounds. "Most marketing students view marketing research as a tedious, meticulous necessity, and not something to be enjoyed," says one experienced market researcher. "But it's the only aspect of marketing that gives us true insight into the minds of consumers, and I find that fascinating."

Pick Your Industry Carefully

Marketers' roles depend greatly on their choice of sector (as described in detail in the "Breakdown by Industry" section). In consumer packaged goods (CPG) companies and agencies, marketers are the market research analysts, brand managers, and VPs of marketing who deliver desirable products to your supermarket shelves and draw your attention to them. In prominent law firms and financial service firms, they are marketing assistants, marketing managers, and chief marketing officers. These firms gain and maintain prominence in an increasingly crowded marketplace for services through adroit service marketing and customer relationship management (CRM). High-tech companies continue to offer positions to specialized marketers who can explain technical advantages in business terms to institutional and consumer clients, and nonprofit organizations are turning to talented and tenacious marketers and fund developers to expand their funding base.

The availability of marketing jobs also depends a great deal on the industry you choose. Business services industries—such as computer and data processing—and management consulting and financial services firms were pinpointed by the U.S. Bureau of Labor Statistics (BLS) as areas of growth in 2003, but the BLS reports that little or no change is expected in manufacturing industries. In a 2003 study, the majority of advertising and marketing professionals surveyed by the Creative Group named pharmaceuticals and biotechnology as the industry most likely to drum up demand for marketing services (23 percent of total), followed closely by the medical and health-care industry (22 percent), then retail and manufacturing (18 percent), and finally business services (16 percent) (The Creative Group, press releases, May 8, 2003, and April 27, 2004). However, some researchers predict a very robust long-term future for business-to-business marketing of goods and services: Estimates range from a conservative $2.7 trillion forecast by Forrester Research to AMR Research's heady prediction of $6 trillion in U.S. volume (Ralph Oliva, "Business-to-Business Marketing Overview," *Marketing News*).

Cause for Cautious Optimism?

Despite all of the gloom and doom of the past few years, the marketing industry may be poised for a modest rebound: Many insiders are predicting there's nowhere for the industry to go but up from here. Some agencies and companies have learned the hard way that cutting out marketing efforts also means cutting into revenues, and are now considering new hires to remedy the situation. A 2004 Creative Group study reveals that 57 percent of advertising and marketing executives expect their company to add marketing and advertising personnel in the coming year, as opposed to 44 percent in 2003. The majority of executives surveyed predicted their hires would be in account management.

The Bottom Line

Make no mistake: There are fewer job openings in marketing now than there were during the '90s boom era. But there are still opportunities to be had—and many argue that the opportunities available today are more solid than those slave-for-stock-options marketing gigs at the dubious dot coms ever were. As long as organizations are in need of funds to run their operations, there will be a need for marketers.

To land any marketing position, you'll need to accumulate significant real-world experience and network extensively. When times get tough, your track record will also be your source of job security. The boom era left behind a glut of self-proclaimed marketers, and your best bet to set yourself apart is to demonstrate analytical skills, creative thinking, and business savvy. Be careful not to overinflate your track record just to get your foot in the door, though—once you've landed your job, you'll be expected to deliver comparable wins for your new employer.

Hiring Trends

According to the 2004–05 Occupational Outlook Handbook from the BLS, overall employment in the field of marketing is expected to increase faster than average—exhibiting a 21 to 35 percent growth—through 2012. The BLS points to growing domestic and global competition in consumer products and services as a key reason for this job growth. However, this growth varies widely by sector: robust growth is anticipated in scientific and professional services realms, while no growth is expected in the manufacturing sector. The BLS also cautions that overall, there will be increased competition for the available full-time opportunities in the field of marketing, especially since hiring contractors is becoming common in lieu of replacing full-time marketing professionals.

This news comes as no surprise to marketers in the field, since few have been spared from widespread layoffs and drastic budget reductions. "It's a massacre out there," says one veteran marketer who's been subjected to three layoffs in the last 3 years. Nonprofit marketers have had to step up their efforts to sustain their organizations, given the shrinking pool of funding available due to government cuts, scarce corporate sponsorships, and decreased individual donations. Many companies have opted to hunker down, keep a low promotional profile, and wait out the recession, which has meant tough times for marketers in many CPG companies and advertising agencies.

But after a few brutal years, marketers' job prospects are beginning to look up, according to the *Wall Street Journal* (Susan McGee, "Recovery Boosts Demand for Marketing Executives," February 10, 2004), and a new survey from the National Association of Colleges and Employers indicates that employers are planning to hire 12.7 percent more new graduates in 2004 than in 2003. Still, according to the 12th annual *Advertising Age* Salary Survey, advertising agencies may require another year before hiring freezes begin to melt and bonuses and other perks begin to surface once again ("The 2003 Advertising Industry Salary Survey," December 8, 2003, www.adage.com).

Breakdown by Industry

Consumer Packaged Goods

CPG marketing is still widely regarded as good core experience for marketers, providing a balance of creative opportunities and analytical rigor to hone marketing skills. CPG marketers can gain a breadth of experience and business skills dealing with cross-functional teams, managing manufacturing and logistics, applying market research findings, and working with creative agencies and other outside vendors.

Insiders say that opportunities are increasingly competitive in the CPG industry, but that they are more consistently available than in other industry segments. As one marketer says, "No matter how bad the economy gets, people still need to eat and clean up after themselves." Top CPG companies include Nestle ($70,823 million in 2003 revenue), Unilever ($53,674 million), Procter & Gamble ($43,377 million), and Kraft Foods ($31,010 million).

One Step Beyond

The conventional wisdom also holds that a broad CPG skill base is a port of entry for consulting or corporate positions in upper management. But experienced marketers caution that CPG marketers should look beyond their narrow product niches to gain the broader market insight and impressive portfolio expected of consultants and executives. "It's helpful if you have a wild card on your resume, especially significant experience at a less conventional, highly regarded consumer branding company with a global presence," says one CPG veteran. "Examples would be a global apparel company such as Nike, or beverage manufacturers like Coke and Pepsi—companies that are image-driven rather than sales-driven."

> **" "**
>
> **It's helpful if you have a wild card on your resume, especially significant experience at a less conventional, highly regarded consumer branding company with a global presence.**

Crash and Burn

CPG marketers are often drawn to multitasking creative positions in brand management and new product development as these offer up the opportunity to develop a broader range of skills and establish a career success record with name brands. But brand managers don't usually get to enjoy their successes for long, since product assignments are turned over every couple of years (if not sooner) to push new products and generate fresh approaches to established brands. Experienced marketers also warn that the constant stress of high-risk, high-visibility campaigns can mean burnout for many brand managers and new product development managers. "The failure rate of new products and brands is high, as is job volatility in these fields," says one insider.

Market Value of Research

Market research is one area within CPG marketing that experts predict will continue to grow, as technology offers access to more specific consumer data and more ways to model consumer behavior. So marketers with a more analytical bent and a desire for a higher degree of stability may choose to specialize in CPG market research. CPG market researchers need to be well-versed in the latest data-gathering technologies, which enable them to survey broad audiences online. At the same time, they have to be comfortable getting very up-close and personal with research subjects. With in-home research, for example, the entire contents of a subject's refrigerator or closet may be discussed in intimate detail, to identify emerging consumer needs and market gaps.

Professional Services

Professional services marketing covers direct-to-consumer services such as insurance, health care, legal assistance, and automotive services, but also services to businesses like business consulting or representation for entertain-ment and sports figures. Finance and technology have spun off from the block of profes-sional services to become distinct industry segments of their own, with defined sets of marketing standards, measures, and consumer behaviors.

Comparing Apples and . . . Apples

One distinct challenge professional services marketers face is that, given the high skill levels often required of specialized service providers, accompanying certification requirements and related government regulations, the differences between service providers may be relatively slight. "If two attorneys have passed the bar exam, the difference between them may not be immediately apparent to the consumer," says one marketer for a legal firm. Marketers are thus faced with differentiating their firm's offerings based on such intangibles as personality, philosophy, and reputation.

Professional Overlap

Marketing positions in a professional services firm may not be housed in a marketing or marcom department at all, but instead may fall under the umbrella of business development or CRM. Professional services marketers within these emerging fields are taking their cue from CPG marketing practices and are moving away from a strictly sales-based model to more of a strategic, analytical approach to anticipating customers' needs with the assistance of analytical frameworks, data sets, and technological tools. Skill sets are thus becoming more transferable between CPG and service marketing. This is good news for marketers who want to keep their career options open. Not that they'd want to make the switch: Service marketers with CRM experience often command higher salaries than do their CPG peers.

Financial Services

From a marketing perspective, financial services has long been considered a more staid, predictable industry segment than higher-risk segments like CPG or technology. Financial firms traditionally emphasize credibility over hype, so marketing has often been treated as essentially a communication function in these enterprises. Financial service marketers are primarily tasked with presenting information on returns and packaging value-added services, while ensuring compliance with disclosure requirements.

Someone Get a Marketer—Stat

In the last few years, however, the financial services arena has proven to be more volatile than predicted. Alleged IPO kickbacks, insider trading, and auditing scandals have tarnished the reputations of once-esteemed financial service companies such as Arthur Andersen (which, due to the Enron scandal, went the way of the dinosaur), Merrill Lynch, Citigroup, and Credit Suisse First

Boston. Established financial services companies must now compete in a more diversified market, where competitors stand to gain from these firms' losses and diminished reputations. For financial service marketers, this means making a stronger case for the value their firms deliver and working harder to establish (or re-establish) firm credibility through increased transparency and reputation management. Some financial services institutions are stepping up their efforts to retain and win individual customers, making increased use of "mystery shoppers" (marketers who go incognito to research customer experience) and new technology to map key markets and identify shifting customer preferences.

Mind the Ethical Minefields

Marketers who do succeed in managing the reputations of financial services companies stand to reap significant rewards and dominate their industry niche. Established financial services marketers are less threatened by up-and-comers, since acquiring the necessary expertise with legal requirements and economic analysis takes considerable time and talent. Tech-savvy marketers are in demand here as in other sectors, but they should proceed with extra caution in the financial services arena. Many customers object to their bank or mortgage company capturing and using their personal financial data for marketing purposes, and legal standards are evolving in this area, too.

"Financial services is a good area for someone who likes a challenge, since restoring both individual and institutional investor confidence will rely in some part on marketing," says one seasoned insider. "But look into your prospective employer's past dealings before you leap. It's an ethical minefield."

Technology

Though the hullabaloo around technology has hushed to a low hum, the field still offers promising opportunities for the enterprising marketer. Biotech pioneers (e.g., Amgen and Genentech), medical technology innovators (e.g., GlaxoSmithKline and 3M's health-care unit), blue-chip tech firms (e.g., Oracle, Microsoft, and IBM) continue to top marketers' lists of companies promising the most career growth. Technology is one field in which headhunters and recruiters continue to compete for marketing talent, attempting to lure the top tech-savvy marketers from tech companies and ad agencies.

Scientifically Speaking

One reason the demand for effective technology marketers remains relatively strong is that the supply is limited. Technology marketing is a specialized field that often demands product-specific and subject-area knowledge, as well as specialized degrees, certifications, and training. Expertise that marketers gain at one technology company is not always transferable to other companies or nontechnology fields—but a marketer with a proven aptitude in any technology field is often highly desirable to a broad range of technology companies and ad agencies. "It's a rare individual who is able to translate complex science into compelling business and consumer terms, and those marketers will always be in demand," says one insider.

Luddites Lose

Marketers should be sensible about which technology companies they join, and take a close look at the company's published financial statements—a little healthy skepticism goes a long way in assessing technology career opportunities. But marketers who are overly skittish about technology firms may miss out on prime career opportunities. The experience of the technology boom has taught many tech companies that a solid business foundation based on consumer understanding is essential to business success—and that makes savvy technology marketers indispensable. "The surviving companies are becoming much more marketing-savvy, which means upcoming demand and new respect for marketers," says one marketing expert.

Nonprofit

Growth potential, decent salaries, adequate budgets, professionalism, transferable skills: These are not terms traditionally associated with marketing in the nonprofit sector. But times have changed, and so have many nonprofits. This expanding sector offers marketers a wealth of career options, valuable experience, and increasingly competitive pay—and of course the opportunity to provide a valued service. True, the incremental average pay increase in the nonprofit sector of 3.6 percent in 2003 may not exactly inspire a happy dance. Planned giving/major gifts officers enjoyed a higher than average raise in 2003 of 6.6 percent, from $56,114 to $59,841, whereas development directors saw their salaries drop $1,436 to $55,569 and chiefs of direct marketing saw their salaries slip 13 percent from $60,515 to $53,359 in 2003 (2004 *NonProfit Times* Salary Survey).

Social Problems R Us

Marketing opportunities in this sector are difficult to characterize, in part because the sector is vast and varied. According to U.S. government figures as of the year 2003, the majority of the organizations that make up the nonprofit sector—including almost one million registered 501(c)(3) nonprofits, plus religious charities and other business-related charitable organizations defined as tax-exempt in the federal tax code—are in health services and education/research, followed by social/legal services, then civic/social/fraternal associations, and finally arts/culture entities. Educational and environmental/animal nonprofits have been the fastest growing areas in the sector in the 1990s. That said, marketers accustomed to large budgets and bonuses or desiring to pay off business school loans quickly will probably find their nonprofit options confined to jobs in the 7,000 or so nonprofit organizations with budgets of $10 million or more—typically educational institutions and hospitals. However, layoffs are occurring across the sector in nonprofits large and small, even among those listed in *NonProfit Times'* 2004 Top 100 list of nonprofits with the highest revenues (for complete list, see www.nptimes.com).

The Incredible Shrinking Budget

Over the past 25 years, shrinking federal budgets and a downward trend in charitable contributions have made marketing a more essential function for many nonprofits. Nonprofit marketers with a strong grasp of business fundamentals and specific experience with fundraising campaigns, database management, grant writing, and partner/donor development are especially valued. Marketers familiar with business-world models of return on investment and efficiency are in demand as nonprofits look to fee-for-service programs and federal, state, and local government grants as their primary funding sources. Skills learned by marketers in the for-profit fields of health-care and legal services marketing are thus becoming more interchangeable with skills of their nonprofit counterparts—and nonprofit salaries in these specialized fields are becoming more competitive, too.

Marketers Make Nice

Marketers crossing over from for-profit fields into the nonprofit sector may have a distinct advantage, but they could be in for a culture shock. Anyone who thrives on competition—as for-profit marketers are encouraged to do—may find themselves temperamentally unsuited to the nonprofit sector, where collaboration is key to effective donor and partner cultivation as well as day-to-day staff management. Marketers may find themselves frustrated with nonprofits' apparent inefficiencies and widespread unfamiliarity with practices taken for granted in the for-profit sector, including accounting, finance, information systems, and advertising.

"They avoid realistically assessing management resources and organizational readiness to meet goals, as though strategic thinking were anathema to goodwill," says one marketer with both nonprofit and for-profit expertise. "But if you can get them to leverage their vision and values effectively, they can be a much more powerful force than any for-profit."

Spanning Industries: Market Research

It doesn't take Einstein to know how to solve any business dilemma at hand, whether it's testing green ketchup, identifying the criteria that inspire clients to switch from a competitor, or identifying issue areas that foundations are most likely to fund. But it does take a savvy market researcher who is able to identify the business problem, the decision alternatives, and the client's needs, and select the appropriate research tools for the task at hand. For example, the audience for online surveys is limited to those with Internet access, and survey subjects tend to be self-selecting and highly opinionated—so this may not be the best way to reach consumers who are on the fence about a particular product choice or to gain insight into the minds of reticent consumers who aren't entirely comfortable with computers.

A market researcher will know the constraints and limitations for each type of survey or test he has to work with, and by using a combination of financial, statistical, scientific, and aesthetic skills, as well as a large dose of common sense, he can and should design an appropriate study that will effectively uncover consumer preferences or needs.

Working the Crowd

Market research firms may also specialize in particular geographic markets, consumer segments, or research tools, such as telephone surveys, focus groups, or online surveys. Companies trying to break into a new market or market segment often get help from a market research firm with proven expertise with that market. To meet these needs, some market research firms specialize in specific legal and business environments (in the European Union, e.g.) or within a certain target consumer segment (such as the U.S. Latino/Hispanic market).

Online Research

Many leading market research firms, such as Forrester Research, Gartner, Zogby International, and Copernicus Marketing Consulting, feature technology-assisted data collection methods in their portfolio of services. In fact, a growing number of research firms are specializing in online surveys, according to *Inside Research*, a newsletter for the market research industry—and with good reason. In 2000, only 10 percent of all market research spending involved Internet surveys, but this is expected to steadily increase to 33 percent by 2006, or about $900 million in expenditures. No wonder three-quarters of all market research firms already have a Web presence (Nancy Beth Jackson, "Opinions to Spare? Click Here," *New York Times*, July 3, 2003). As of July 2002, 20 percent of all quantitative research was being conducted online, and the figure is expected to continue to increase at a rate of 50 percent through 2005 (*Inside Research*, July 2002).

Companies leading the pack in online surveys include Harris Interactive, Nielsen//NetRatings, SurveyMonkey, AOL, Zoomerang, and SurveyGold, but stay tuned for breaking developments—market research firms may be in the business of making predictions, but these days they also seem to be in the business of breaking them.

Spam Alert!

But not all firms that call themselves "online research firms" are legitimate. Some are thinly disguised spam factories, e-mailing and posting banner ad "surveys" that reward respondents with a lifetime of e-mails about diet supplements, no-money-down mortgages, and various contraptions that promise everything short of eternal life with regular usage. If you think there's no harm done by spam, think again: According to Ferris Research, U.S. companies will have to spend more than $10 billion this year in cash and wasted time cleaning up after spammers, and Gartner reports that about $2 of your usual monthly Internet service fees goes to fighting spam. As well, Symantec estimates that 47 percent of children have received spam with X-rated links.

Your Name on the Line Online

Spam is a lucrative business, and it does take a certain strategic acumen—but it does not qualify as true market research, because it does not seek to strategically identify and meet a consumer or client need with appropriate research methods. The mass e-mail approach is a given, and the strategy is always a variation on the same pie-in-the-face approach: Hurl messages in the general direction of consumers until something sticks. So not only is the practice of spamming offensive to businesses, consumers, and kids, it's also an insult to the intelligence and intentions of any true market researcher. Be sure to ask about the privacy standards and practices of any market research firm where you're seriously considering a job—after all, it's your professional reputation on the line.

Trends in the Field

More with Less

This field has always required fast thinking and fancy footwork, but in a tougher economy the strategic and creative demands of the field have become still more strenuous. Efficiency measures have led to resource-slashing that makes it harder for marketers to be effective. For example, in its 1999 analysis of 183 companies in periods of recession and recovery, the U.K.-based Profit Impact of Marketing Strategy found that 110 of those companies cut ad expenditures—even though these budget savings tended to result in sluggish corporate growth over the long term.

Marketing vs. Marcom

The multitasking necessitated by budget-slashing measures also gives more people some claim to marketing expertise—"Everyone thinks they're marketers nowadays," says one longtime marketer—so the pool of marketing talent is heavily diluted with people whose primary expertise is sales, public relations, or some other business discipline grouped under the nebulous title of "marcom." But skilled marketers with proven success demonstrated by profit margins, market share, quantifiable boosts to reputation, and other measurable (read: quantifiable) gains are still first in line to win key positions with leading organizations. The difference between marketing and marcom, ultimately, is in the numbers.

Finding Methods to the Madness

Like any other marketers, market researchers are in high-pressure positions where they are expected to increase profit margins, and they feel the pinch when marketing budgets are tight—after all, if there are no plans for ambitious marketing campaigns, there isn't such a burning need for market research. Research budgets are also cut to the quick, which can make it difficult for marketers and market researchers alike to get to know their audience—and prove their worth in delivering quantifiable gains. "Not long ago, we had the budget to do extensive audience surveys in all of our geographic target markets to inform our strategies," says one insider. "Now I'm lucky if senior management will cough up for a focus group. How am I supposed to show widespread, measurably improved brand recognition with a single focus group? The evidence is all anecdotal."

Finding a Silver Lining in Research

For the most part, the trends in market research are consistent with the rest of the industry: not-so-hot job outlook, emphasis on faster/cheaper methods, and increasing reliance on technology to deliver results cost-effectively. Market researchers are now expected to continually upgrade their technical skills; this may entail a significant investment in training at the graduate or even doctoral level. But the data and analytical insight market researchers deliver are understood as having intrinsic long-term learning value for an organization apart from sales figures. This is different from marketers who are charged with defining creative approaches, which may take just as much effort to develop but are judged more narrowly by sales results.

Starting at the Bottom

Marketers across the board should set their sights on realistic job targets. MBAs with some experience who may have entered grad school expecting to land brand manager positions may have to lobby all of their B-school contacts to score a position as marketing assistant or assistant brand manager, and work their way up to brand manager. Undergrads with some experience may find themselves jockeying to become unpaid or underpaid ad agency interns, and may remain interns for much longer than they'd expected. Even midcareer hires making the move to marketing with the help of contacts should be prepared to assume entry-level positions, and certainly take a hit in pay for at least the first few years. Executives hoping to shift to the marketing side of their organizations should know that during an economic slump, there's a good chance they'll be edged out by marketers brought from outside with a proven track record of financial wins—and lower salary expectations.

Ethical Quandaries

With stiffer competition for minimal marketing opportunities that pale in comparison to the boom years of 1999 and 2000, the question may come up sooner rather than later: Just how far are you willing to go to get ahead in marketing? In the course of your career, your personal values may well be put to the test by any of the following ethical quandaries reported by experienced marketers:

- Shilling tobacco products, alcoholic beverages, diet drugs, steroids, or other products that are potentially hazardous to consumers' health.

- Spamming e-mail users with test messages under the dubious premise of "online consumer research," for a client that is charging exorbitant prices for a pill that allegedly cures erectile dysfunction.

- Peddling stuff to small children, whose beleaguered parents may curse you whenever their kids beg for your product in the supermarket.

- Hawking accounting services for a firm with a less-than-sterling reputation.

- Promoting casinos or online gambling sites.

- Capturing private financial data of mortgage company clients for marketing purposes, knowing full well that this data may eventually be sold to direct marketing firms.

- Hyping ambulance-chasing lawyers.

- Seeking regulatory roadblocks to the development of generic alternatives to a life-saving drug, so that your company's patented version keeps its market monopoly.

- Doctoring up "actual" before-and-after shots for a plastic surgery ad.

- Drumming up business for a hardcore porn website, magazine, or video business.

As a marketer, you should know where you stand on these ethical issues *before* they arise in the course of your business dealings—and before a potential employer springs an ethical question on you in an interview. If you want to have a marketing career that will do you proud, first be honest with yourself about what you are—and aren't—willing to do, and then make your career decisions accordingly.

Marketing Myth-Busting

When it comes to identifying prime opportunities, conventional wisdom often needs to be turned on its head. The CPG industry has long been considered a launching pad for marketers, but ambitious marketers may need to go elsewhere to find the breadth of experience and opportunity they require for career advancement. Marketers hoping to make a name for themselves often aim for brand management positions at places like Procter & Gamble and Nestle, but affiliation with a brand name may in the long run provide less job security than solid work experience in marketing research or advanced expertise (including graduate degrees) in specialized scientific, technology, or services industry segments. Service marketing looks more like CPG marketing and less like a traditional sales model, given its strategic orientation toward customer needs. With the continued growth of online research and cutting-edge data collection methods, new name-brand market research firms are enlivening a sector long associated with data-crunching drudgery. Financial services marketing is no longer the stable, risk-averse field it once was, while nonprofits can offer longer-term career stability for resourceful marketers who have a knack for fee-for-service marketing, corporate sponsorships, and grant writing.

On the Job

- The Big Picture

- Marketing Associate/Brand Assistant

- Brand/Product Manager

- Creative Specialist

- Marketing/Fund Development Director

- Market Researcher

- Marketing Consultant

The Big Picture

Marketers keep the inventors of career aptitude assessment tests like Myers-Briggs up at night, defying test typologies with their statistically unlikely combination of abilities in analysis and creativity, intuition and logic, people skills, and comfort with numbers. "Marketers think with their left and right brains in equal proportions," says one veteran insider. "They can understand numbers and people," adds another. "They listen for subtexts when people talk, and are able to interpret people's emotions; this is what drives people to become marketers and makes them good at what they do. Marketers have to identify what people are implicitly saying but not explicitly stating, and deliver against those needs."

To understand consumer motivations and behavior, marketers need to be able to identify strongly with their consumers. "You can't be a good marketer unless you can put yourself in the position of a potential or current customer and ask yourself and your company the question, 'What could you do to better fit my needs?'" says one insider. This requires you as a marketer not only to make leaps of logic from data you've collected, but also leaps of imagination from the comfort of your office into the mind of, say, a 10-year-old girl in Atlanta, Georgia. "Any brand has to know consumers better than they know themselves," says one insider. This entails knowledge of your target consumer's personal goals as well as purchasing goals. As one marketing executive says, "You need to recognize that when they walk up to the register, consumers are not just making purchase decisions, but life decisions." Some specific job responsibilities are outlined in the following "A Day in the Life" profiles (Note: These profiles are composites, with product names and industry details altered to protect the anonymity of profiled marketers, their employers, and coworkers.)

The following are among the most commonly cited basic qualifications for marketers:

- Multitasking

- Opportunity analysis and assessment

- Financial management

- Creative development and implementation

- Research

- Brand development

- Product development

- Leadership

- Empathy

- Ability to integrate quantitative and qualitative criteria

- Good interpersonal skills

- Curiosity

- Self-awareness

Marketers think with their left and right brains in equal proportions. They can understand numbers and people.

On the Job

Marketing Associate/Brand Assistant

Pay attention whenever someone on the marketing team uses the word *tracking*, because as a marketing associate (in tech or professional services circles) or brand assistant (in CPG jargon), this means work for you. You'll be responsible for conducting the research your company uses to plan its strategies and gauge its marketing successes, including market analysis, competitive analysis, monitoring promotional campaigns, and tracking sales and market share numbers. For this, you'll need a background in statistics, research method-ologies, data analysis, and interpretation—and of course, the presentation and communication skills to explain these numbers in a succinct and meaningful way. Familiarity with finance and accounting practices is helpful, since you'll be budgeting and monitoring expenditures, too. All told, be prepared to work 45 to 65 hours per week, or until the numbers start to blur.

Typical Responsibilities

Typical responsibilities include the following:

- Data tracking, analysis, interpretation, and presentation
- Budget management
- Sundry office tasks related to marketing, however tangentially:
    - Database management
    - Proofing ad copy and reports
    - Running interference with vendors
    - E-mailing meeting notes to participants
    - Project management

The Upside

The pay is much less than ideal, but the experience you pick up in this position can pay off in the long run. If you're working in an advertising agency or a CPG company with multiple product lines in the same category, you may have the opportunity to work on several brands and build a nice portfolio in the process. You may pick up some useful technology skills, such as database management or website usage tracking.

Furthermore, you may be invited—or even required—to attend market research and sales seminars in-house and in the field. True, all those conferences in Kansas City may cramp your social life—but it's always wise to learn on someone else's dime, plus you'll make some contacts in the field that could come in handy when you're ready to move up in the world.

A Day in the Life of a Marketing Associate/Brand Assistant

8:00   Check e-mail and ongoing project timelines on company's project management software; notice that budgets are due in 2 weeks. E-mail boss (again) this quarter's actuals, along with a gentle prod about getting that budget to me in time to proof.

9:00   Check in with vendor to ensure shipment of promotional fridge magnets was delivered to retailers as scheduled. Magnets were indeed delivered—the wrong ones though. Move into crisis management mode. After half an hour wrangling with the vendor on the phone, vendor agrees to deliver correct magnets, pick up wrong ones at no cost, and absorb production and warehousing costs. This is a victory, but only a short-lived one; now that I know that my vendor is unreliable, I'll have to research new ones.

10:00 Call retailers and explain situation; while on the phone with one retailer, discover that a competitor's cookies are flying off the shelves. Make note to suggest competitive analysis of that product in weekly team meeting.

11:30 Adjust expenditures to reflect anticipated reduced cost of fridge magnets; approve pile of invoices and enter them on expenditures spreadsheet.

12:30 Hike over to the neighborhood food court with a couple of other assistants; run into harried boss, who asks that I forward this quarter's actuals. Tactfully suggest that my boss check this morning's e-mail; receive grateful smile from boss and sympathetic eye-roll from fellow assistants.

1:30 Run reports of Glinty dishwashing soap promotional website usage; notice that click-through rate from banner ad placed on NewYorkTimes.com over the last quarter exceeds 0.2 percent, while all others fall far short of the 0.1 percent projected. Notice that NewYorkTimes.com readers are twice as likely to proceed to sign up for promotional giveaways and e-mail lists. Check with two assistants working on other brands, who report similar findings for those brands.

3:30 Boss calls asking me to photocopy actuals for marketing team meeting on Web promotional expenditures; word has come down from on high that next year's budget for Web promotions will be cut 50 percent. I'm invited to sit in on the meeting to take notes, and perk up when someone mentions slashing all banner ads. I pipe up with my findings about NewYorkTimes.com banner ads. The marketing director asks me to investigate banner ads further, and report back directly to her with my findings.

5:00 Write up action items from meeting, and e-mail to all participants.

6:00 Catch up on work e-mail; scan Web to price fridge magnets from alternate vendors.

7:00 Carpool home with a marketing researcher I've been getting to know, who congratulates me on my banner ad observations and hints that there might be an opening for a Web-savvy researcher on the market research side.

Brand/Product Manager

If the prospect of juggling torches doesn't scare you, you'll thrive at brand management. Brand and product managers are said to "own" a particular brand or product within a company's or consulting firm's portfolio and are personally responsible for every conceivable aspect of that brand as well as its overall success. In a day's work, brand and product managers may juggle forecasting, product development, manufacturing, testing, packaging, trademark protections, budgeting, promotions, and advertising. New product development (NPD) managers, an offshoot of brand management, are responsible for taking a product from its very first appearance as a promising idea through to its appearance in a consumer's shopping cart.

NPD and brand managers must excel at teamwork and leadership, because there are not enough hours in the day to personally micromanage every aspect of a brand. Often brand managers have MBAs, and companies are increasingly hiring brand managers from within their ranks of experienced assistant brand managers and brand assistants with considerable experience and an MBA. You'll need at least 5 years of experience to qualify for a brand management position, and should expect to work 45 to 60 hours per week.

Typical Responsibilities

Typical responsibilities include the following:

- R&D
- Production
- Packaging

- Distribution
- Advertising
- Promotion
- New product development and testing
- Financial and volume forecasting
- Budget and profit/loss management
- Trademark and copyright management

The Upside

While it may seem confining to be attached to a particular brand, brand management is a launching pad to a number of possible careers. Ambitious brand and product managers may move up the ranks at CPG companies, or opt to work in consumer goods groups at larger consulting firms like Booz Allen, McKinsey, and Monitor. Brand management attracts budding entrepreneurs for a reason, says one brand manager: "It's a good way to cultivate a range of expertise from production through sales, and to develop the business skills you would need to launch your own company."

A Day in the Life of a Brand Manager

8:00   Sift through e-mail inbox full of sales reports, expenditure reports, reports comparing cost projections to actuals. Wasn't it just budget time last month?

9:00   Meet with market research consultant, R&D specialist, and manufacturing rep to discuss findings on nut butters. Surveys suggest moms want "health-conscious" chunky nut butter, but taste testing reveals that they prefer sugar-added nut butters and dislike natural oil separation. Request further research on market for vitamin-fortified spreads and on blending processes that leave chunkiness intact.

10:30   Assistant brand manager comes by to get sign-off on a label change I haven't had a chance to look over. Go over the rationale for the change and the associated costs; I agree with the need for design change, but I'm not convinced about costly changes to the color scheme. Ask assistant brand manager to modify design, sticking to current color scheme.

11:30   Check in with ad agency about to cast all-important role of mom for series of commercials. Recall that new research findings show more affluent moms identify with older women; advise agency to look for an older actor than the one they cast last time.

12:00   E-mail from brand assistant. Have I looked at budget projections and actuals yet? After lunch, I promise.

12:30   Lunch with brand manager assigned to butter substitute brand I managed for 2 years, before my promotion to the leading peanut butter brand. New findings on cholesterol levels in butter substitutes have hurt the market (I got out just in time). Cheer up unfortunate brand manager, and help brainstorm promotional ideas.

1:45   Back to conference call with heads of sales, new product development, and market research on sales of peanut butter in squeeze bottles (patent pending). It's selling well in the Midwest, but sales have been disappointing in the Northeast despite promising survey data. Agree focus groups are needed to gain better understanding of divergent consumer response. Note to self on PDA: Check with legal about that patent. . . .

3:45   Back to e-mail. Supply chain manager alerts me: Paper prices are about to go up again. Forward message to brand assistant with request to run price comparisons from various vendors and factor price hikes into budget. Good thing I didn't sign off on those numbers.

4:15   Look over media plan for new commercial; determine I could cut back on Web advertising and beef up television coverage in selected markets. E-mail note to assistant brand manager to run cost/benefit analysis.

6:15   Switch gears; make notes on status reports from assistant brand managers for weekly team status meeting tomorrow morning.

7:00   Think about going to gym, but head home instead. I dodged the budget bullet today, but it'll catch up with me tomorrow. . . .

Creative Specialist

Many marketers find they particularly enjoy the creative side of marketing and brand development, such as brand or corporate identity development, packaging, or copywriting. You don't need an MBA or any other special credential to move into the creative side beyond excellent, proven creative and problem-solving skills—a combination that is not always so easy to come by. In addition to striking visual abilities or a distinctive flair for writing—talents that some in the industry claim you have to be born with—you'll need to be an extremely patient, analytical observer of human behavior and industry trends to know what will work to win customers away from the competition.

Insiders say that in a tight economy, the competition is especially fierce for customer dollars even for creative specialists with impressive portfolios: "No one can afford to lose a client, so you'll need to bring your A game to work every single day," says one copywriter. Since the barriers to entry are relatively low, there are always new people entering the field eager to establish themselves (and possibly replace you) with low rates, long hours, and dubious credentials. As the saying goes in many creative specialist fields, "You are only as good as your last campaign"; these fields are rife with burnout and spectacular falls from grace. The working hours are part of the problem: Expect to work 50- to 75-hour weeks.

Typical Responsibilities

Typical responsibilities include the following:

- Niche specialization: copywriting, production, art direction (note: in most cases, the more specialized you are, the better your career prospects will be)
- Project planning and management

- Creative presentation of concept, strategies, and executions
- Client development (a must for consultants and many agencies)
- Competitive research
- Assessing advertising and promotional campaigns to gauge success and learn

The Upside

These are legitimate and potentially lucrative fields in their own right; ad agency copywriters, commercial video/film producers and other "creatives" with a track record of successful campaigns can command salaries that rival those of marketing directors and even VPs. Many enterprising creatives also start their own agencies or independent consulting practices. Although not all succeed financially despite putting in long hours of work, self-promotion, and business management, for some the sheer volume of work is a fair tradeoff for the flexibility that allows them to pick their kids up from school, take a walk, or wear pajamas all day.

A Day in the Life of a Creative Specialist

8:00   Get up; head to gym for an hour; shower; take off for work.

9:30   Roll into work; consume first of many cups of coffee over e-mail. Get comments from the account manager about Swell Computers account; they loved the concept, but are looking for "something a little different" to make the ad "skew younger, without being sophomoric." Try not to take this as an insult; call account manager for specifics. Are they talking teens? Tweens? No details to be had.

10:00   Do research on Web; discover Swell has been losing market share to Moonbeam Computers, especially in college student market. Check out Moonbeam computer collateral; notice new flat screen and tagline, "Get hip to the screen." That's going to be a tough one to beat.

11:30   Re-read brand promise, key messages, selling points of Swell computers. Makes sense—but how do I make teenagers care about what Swell has to say? What do they care about?

12:00 Colleague solicits feedback on candy bar ad; catches me checking out teen movie sites and chat rooms; raises eyebrow. "Research," I say. Notice sci-fi movies losing popularity—so much for that alien concept. Discover '80s are back, but another computer company is already using '80s music in ads.

1:00 Dejected; head for lunch alone. Wonder if I'm losing my edge. There's been talk of more layoffs around the agency due to limited new business; I can't afford to bring Swell anything less than stellar copy. Call my sister to commiserate; college-age nephew Trevor answers while watching *Fast Times at Ridgemont High*—"It's a classic, dude." That gets me thinking. . . .

1:45 Rush back; scan Web for Jeff Spicoli, surfers, surfing.

2:30 Tear myself away for new client meeting; account manager does all of the talking. Introduced as genius behind Swell computer ads—no pressure or anything . . .

3:45 Head back to computer; read rave teen reviews of new surfing blockbuster. Find surfing slang dictionary. Swell means wave. "Surf the Swell" could work. . . .

5:30 Do a search; discover "Surf the Swell" is trademarked tagline of *Swell Surfing* magazine. Too bad!

6:00 Check e-mail; find reminder about follow-up meeting with client in hair transplant business tomorrow. Must get cracking on concept.

8:30 Head home, resolving to get a head start on the hair transplant concept tomorrow. Hey, "Get a head start" could work. . . .

Marketing/Fund Development Director

If you're aiming to become a captain of industry or a nonprofit mover and shaker, a marketing director position is one big step in the right direction. An MBA from a well-regarded school may be helpful in getting you in the door—particularly if there are fellow alumni at your target organization—but it's by no means a guarantee that you'll be seriously considered as a candidate for this position.

To land this job, you'll need 5 to 8 years of experience within a particular industry, with a solid track record of successful launches and relaunches of products or service offerings—plus the numbers to back up your claims. On the nonprofit side, you'll need to show significant gains in donations, sponsorships, grants, or fee-for-service client rosters to become a marketing director or director of development. You'll need strong team-building and management experience to see your team through setbacks, inspiring them to defy the odds with spectacular marketing successes. This effort will take 50 to 75 hours a week, or until you've accomplished your marketing goals.

Typical Responsibilities

Typical responsibilities include the following:

- Strategy development
- Managing portfolio of brands (or fund development efforts: annual fund drive, corporate sponsorships, grant proposals, etc.)

- Budget allocation and oversight

- Managing team of marketing, product, fund development or brand managers and assistants

- Business unit profit and loss management and accountability

The Upside

The contacts you make and cement in your role as marketing director are powerful—and portable. On the job, you'll develop strong relationships with key players in ad agencies, the media, consulting firms, your industry, and the marketing field in general. These professional contacts will link you to the services, people, ideas, and exposure you and your organization need to make your marketing program a success. When you move on to greener pastures, you'll take a much weightier address book with you—in fact, that address book probably helped you land your new job in the first place. If you tend to them with care over time, your relationships will give you the inside track on prime marketing positions before they're ever made public. Membership in a professional association like the American Marketing Association is one way to cultivate these relationships outside your organization, as is attendance at marketing and industry conferences.

A Day in the Life of a Marketing Director

8:00   Check e-mail; review schedule and progress reports on project management timeline; look over Thrive tracksuit brand extension plan.

9:30   Begin SWOT (strength, weakness, opportunities, threats) analysis on Thrive running shoes. Pull down public sales data from competitors; notice running shoe market seems to be down overall, while sales are up for orthopedic walking shoes. Interesting . . .

11:00   Run across news article about strike at plant in Indonesia where my company sources shoelaces. Turns out strike is about working conditions; recall recent child labor scandal about competitor shoe manufacturer led to boycott and bad press. Forward article to VP of marketing and head of PR, along with note recommending conference call with operations researcher and key supplier in region to assess situation and need for damage control. VP agrees; call is scheduled.

11:30 Clarify points of strategy with brand manager on tracksuit brand extension plan. I'm not convinced that product placements in rap videos are the right vehicle to convey Thrive's message to suburban women aged 25 to 35, which is currently the fastest-growing market segment in this area; we briefly brainstorm together and decide to look into product placements in movies and television programs aimed at this segment instead.

12:15 Lunch (sandwiches again) over meeting with VPs of marketing and sales to review quarterly results against projections. Discussion on strategic priorities ensues. As I'm heading back to my office, I notice an *O* magazine article on a brand assistant's desk on "gearing up to get in shape." That gets me thinking: It would be great if we could somehow arrange a giveaway of tracksuits to Oprah's studio audience as a tie-in to a get-in-shape episode. . . .

3:15 Review agency creative for upcoming shoe campaign, along with manager's recommendations.

3:45 Brand manager back for signoff on amended Thrive tracksuit brand extension plan. I send an e-mail to friends and colleagues to ask if anyone knows a PR consultant with success putting clients in touch with Oprah, or has any personal experience with giveaways on "Oprah" and might be willing to share tips or advice.

4:30 Conference call on Indonesian plant strike. Information-gathering reveals supplier in question thwarted official inspections of facilities in past, but denies increasingly frequent reports of deteriorating working conditions. Team resolves to pressure supplier to agree to labor union demands, while seeking alternative suppliers and issuing press statement of company's determination to work only with suppliers with working conditions that exceed industry standards. VP marketing praises me for bringing matter to senior management's attention.

6:45 I've got e-mail: A former colleague I had lunch with last Tuesday has e-mailed me back, saying that her sister-in-law works at Oprah's Harpo Productions and might be able to tell me who to talk to about a giveaway; e-mail profuse thanks and insist on treating to lunch next week.

7:00 Checking over schedule, respond to e-mails from managers and ad agency requesting follow-up meetings and strategy planning meetings. E-mail brand manager with few additional questions on shoe campaign creative.

7:30 Remember those orthopedic walking shoes; fire off e-mail to market research to collect data on exercise trends, particularly walking.

8:00 Decide to get home and take a walk—in my Thrive athletic shoes, of course.

Market Researcher

If the word "triangulation" is music to your ears, you may have a future in market research. While brand assistants and marketing associates are often handed the task of number crunching and data analysis, the actual research design is typically a job for expert market researchers. This field requires sharp analytical skills and a keen eye for data patterns that could point the way to effective product development and promotional strategies. You will also need to get comfortable—if not intimately familiar—with software used in market research, especially the following:

- SPSS for statistical analysis
- Sawtooth for conjoint analysis
- CATI for sample selection
- Web data analysis software such as Accrue or WebTrends

CRM applications are also useful to know, since researchers familiar with CRM methodologies often command higher salaries. A PhD in marketing—or other discipline requiring strong communication and analytical skills such as psychology, sociology, politics, IT, math, or English literature—is helpful for career advancement, but an MBA or an MA in statistical analysis with a background in psychology or anthropology may get you in the door. Over time, you might begin to specialize in a specific industry, type of research (e.g., focus groups, interviewing, online surveys), or market segment (tweens, Hispanic/Latino, gay/lesbian). If your research specialty is particularly in demand, you might get snapped up by a market research firm or decide to start your own consultancy. Effective market researchers are naturally curious about people, and are quick to pick up on peculiar coincidences and intriguing idiosyncrasies—making them invaluable in the marketplace and great at cocktail parties. Your hours will range from 35 to 65 a week.

Typical Responsibilities

Typical responsibilities include the following:

- Researching project design—methodology, metrics, sample selection
- Conducting surveys, new product tests, polls, focus groups, in-home or in-store interviews and relational research (i.e., Nielsen ratings)
- Data collection, tabulation, analysis, and presentation
- Assessing effectiveness of advertising and promotional campaigns (especially in ad agencies)
- Making recommendations to manufacturing and sales forces about the market for their product
- Product R&D and testing

The Upside

Research design is often misunderstood as being a dull, uncreative discipline, a tedious process of matching questions about the marketplace with appropriate methodologies, samples, and metrics. But creative thinking is required to produce the most insightful qualitative and quantitative data on consumer behavior, and the process of market research can be anything but dull. Think of coolhunters, the market researchers who identify emerging trends through contextual studies of trendsetters, or applied anthropologists, who uncover unmet needs through participant observation with a target consumer group. Many researchers are independent consultants, academics, or they work for ad agencies or market research firms. They get the inside scoop on a much broader range of consumers, companies, and brands in a single year than pigeonholed brand managers might in a lifetime. Brand managers may gloat that they get free dinners with ad execs, but just remember: They'll still be talking about shampoo while you're dashing off to run a pharmaceutical focus group in Brazil.

A Day in the Life of a Market Researcher

8:00   Sort through e-mails; find an urgent message from a new assistant brand manager of Zeroes cereal at client company Frankenstuff, panicked about the results of a cereal category analysis I conducted that is about to be sent to partner retailers. These findings show last quarter's category leader, Zeroes, trailing a distant fifth after rival brands. I set up a time to meet with the assistant brand manager.

9:00   Spend some time preparing for that evening's focus group on nut butters. Give final once-over to questions; add in a few pertinent psychographic probes. What is it that inspires consumers to branch out from peanut butter and try almond butter instead? Can they be convinced to switch to cashew butter, too? Inquiring minds want to know—and so does my client, who dominates the non-peanut nut-butter market, and sold 2.7 times more almond butter than cashew butter last year.

10:30   Interrupted by a call from the marketing director at Frankenstuff who's also alarmed by the category analysis and baffled that several of the company's brands seem to have performed poorly against generic private label/store brands last quarter. Could I produce a top-line summary comparing recent results from private label and Frankenstuff brands? Quickly compile requested data into graphs; notice steep drop-off in Frankenstuff sales across all price points against private labels in December—a time of year when Frankenstuff brands had historically been strong. Hmm . . .

12:30   Lunchtime; head out to lunch with a tech-savvy marketing assistant I'm grooming for an analyst position on the market research team. Interesting conversation about the future of collaborative filtering software ensues. Can a simple online quiz identifying a consumer's taste in music be used to reveal what flavor of soda that consumer is likely to drink? Sounds like science fiction, but the assistant tells me the software has been in development for 5 years. Make mental note to add scan for "collaborative filtering" to my online article tracking service.

1:30   Back to work wrapping up last-minute focus group issues. Brief the interviewers on changes to the questions; go over focus group preparations with marketing analysts.

2:30   Meet with Frankenstuff's troubled assistant brand manager, who wants to drop the new category leader, WheatSmart, out of the category research portfolio as an "outlier" to make Zeroes look better. Gently remind the wet-behind-the-ears assistant brand manager that these findings must be included to maintain credibility with the partner retail chain; suggest running competitive intelligence study on marketing patterns of competitor brands since last quarter to identify winning strategies. Will I help? Of course.

3:00   Look over top-level comparison of private-label and Frankenstuff brands; write up executive summary drawing attention to peculiar drop-off in performance in December.

5:00   On my way to the focus group, drop off the report to the marketing director at Frankenstuff. Casually ask, "Is there any common denominator you can imagine affecting these brands in December?" When the marketing director blanches, suddenly I remember: Several experienced brand managers and assistant brand managers were laid off at Frankenstuff in December. Offer that the CPG marketing practice at my consulting firm could train new hires. Could I set that up right away? Of course. Conference in an account manager; exit to sounds of deal being hammered out.

6:00   Observe focus group; learn that moms consider nut butters with a slight grain "healthier." Belly growls—resolve never to do another focus group on an empty stomach.

8:00   Head home to fix my kids cashew butter sandwiches for tomorrow's lunch with leftover focus group freebies.

Marketing Consultant

Up for a challenge? Once you've acquired specialized skills, strategic acumen, and a list of impressive accomplishments with well-known brands or organizations with contacts to match, you may be ready to get out from under the corporate (or nonprofit) umbrella and enter the world of consulting. Most successful marketing consultants have experience at the marketing director or VP level, with a minimum of 8 years of experience in marketing and a broad range of expertise and success stories to show for it. Some choose to sign on with established consulting firms, where they get to work with a broader range of brands, services, and organizations than they would in a corporation—but without losing the benefits and steady income to which they've become accustomed. Going into business with a partner is one way to hedge your bets; you might team up with a market researcher to become a one-stop marketing strategy shop.

Other brave souls decide to go it alone as independent consultants, putting the business skills they've acquired as marketers to the ultimate test of running their own business. Keep in mind that as an independent consultant, you'll need to absorb the costs of your own benefits, accounting, marketing efforts, legal fees, business website development, promotional materials, and business losses from delinquent clients—and suddenly, that attractive hourly rate may look a lot less attractive than a salary at a consulting firm. "You have to be your own rainmaker," says one insider with 10 years' experience as a consultant. Consultants with firms may work 50 to 70 hours per week. The sky's the limit for independent consultants just starting out, but 60 to 75 hours per week is not unusual after the first year or two.

Typical Responsibilities

Typical responsibilities include the following:

- Market research and forecasting
- Industry and competitive analysis
- Systems assessment and troubleshooting
- Data collection and analysis
- Training
- Supply chain management
- Market performance assessment and recommendations
- Advertising and cross-platform promotional program development
- Product testing

The Upside

As a consultant, all of those research methods courses you took and that statistical modeling software you learned as an analyst are about to come in handy. Since clients often hire them to handle the difficult work of market and business systems analysis, consulting firms may well be scanning your resume for solid quantitative skills, savvy research applications, and statistical software proficiency. Market research skills will help you command more money and respect as an independent consultant, too. If research is not your forte, consider partnering with an experienced market researcher to broaden your service offerings, and increase your competitive advantage. If you back your campaign strategy with solid research, you'll be taken much more seriously by your clients.

A Day in the Life of a Marketing Consultant

9:00   Over cereal, check my PDA for appointments and reminders. Walk to office in fuzzy slippers (it's just downstairs); go through e-mail. Caterer I met at alumni mixer wants to know my rates. E-mail nice note and link to my website; offer to cost out the project—"I'm sure we can work something out," I say.

10:30   Follow-up call from prospective client where I just submitted a bid on a wedding planning promotional project. They liked the proposal, but want to know if I could go any lower on my bid. Discuss options; they mention website redevelopment could be put off until next quarter, and still be completed before wedding planning season begins in earnest. I offer to rework my bid without the website piece, and submit it again.

11:00   Rework bid; fire it off with winsome cover note.

12:30   Contact copywriter I subcontracted to write media kit for upscale restaurant chain. Now they want an invite for an upcoming black-tie benefit. Copywriter is leaving on vacation next week and isn't available. Looks like my weekend is now spoken for.

1:00   Over hastily assembled sandwich, decide to get cracking on the invite. Take out brochure as point of reference; start brainstorming concepts.

2:30   Check e-mail; find note from editor of food industry magazine I pitched an article to a couple of weeks ago. Editor wants me to write a story on resurgence of comfort foods. Do victory dance—the pay is negligible, but the exposure in my industry niche is invaluable.

3:00   Get follow-up call from caterer; his project is a promotional brochure he wants done in 3 weeks, in time for a food fair. Gently break news to him about printing timelines; suggest elegant card instead. Could I send him an estimate for the card? No problem.

3:30   Call printer and graphic designer, pull together estimate, send to caterer.

4:00   Get to work on promotional strategy for baking company—the client who recommended me to the wedding planner. Make note to send gift basket to bakers if wedding planner gig works out.

6:00   Come out of my office for quick jog, shower, and dinner with significant other (takeout again).

8:00   Retreat again to work on that invite.

9:30   Add up billable hours: 5 hours. Not great, but I've had worse. I deserve a video.

The Workplace

- Culture and Lifestyle

- Workplace Diversity

- Compensation

- Career Opportunities

- Insider Scoop

Culture and Lifestyle

The general public thinks of marketing as a creative field where unconventional thinking and attitudes reign supreme—but marketers know better. There is no one culture of marketing that applies across all organizations, and many departments would hardly be described as freewheeling. Marketing departments in some conservative CPG companies are often as straight-laced, buttoned-down, hierarchical, and analytical as the rest of the company. Even marketing departments that initially seem chaotic and nontraditional—such as those often found in tech companies or nonprofits—may operate according to an established set of strategic priorities not apparent to the casual visitor.

"There are no generalizations when it comes to marketing departments," says one insider. "Each organization has its own culture, which is often dictated from top down. Marketing departments range from conservative and risk-averse to very progressive and open to new directions. Do your homework on a company, so you know what you're getting yourself into culturally."

By Industry

Marketers often characterize marketing departments according to industry.

Consumer Packaged Goods

CPG companies are categorized as more conservative in culture, with hierarchical structures, dress codes, and long-established internal systems. This perception is heightened by the location of many CPG headquarters in smaller U.S. cities and towns between the coasts—for example, Procter & Gamble is in Cincinnati, Ohio, and General Mills is in St. Louis, Missouri. "Location is the worst thing about CPG," says one longtime CPG insider who prefers metropolitan living on the coasts. CPG companies draw employees from around the nation and globe and are often located in the heartland primarily because of the cost savings—but the perception remains that these middle-American CPG companies are homogenous and change-resistant.

Financial Services

Financial services companies are also characterized as conservative, due in part to more traditional business dress codes and rigid working hours that typically coincide with the open and close of the New York Stock Exchange. But the practice of marketing within these organizations can be anything but cut-and-dried. "It's intellectually challenging to understand customer motivations and responses, given the inherently abstract nature of services," says one insider. "So the job can be creative and fun." These companies tend to be located in major urban centers along the coasts and in Chicago, and are accordingly fast-paced. However, the culture of these companies may shift with its fortunes in the market. One noted financial services company hired in-house massage therapists and chiropractors during the heady boom era—then promptly laid them off when the market started to nosedive.

Nonprofit

In the nonprofit sector, you won't ever have to worry about getting too used to in-house massage therapists—for the most part, nonprofits earn their reputation for long hours, close quarters, and low pay. However, many nonprofits are not as strapped for cash as you might think. According to the National Center for Charitable Statistics, there are almost 300,000 registered public charities who filed IRS receipts in 2004, and together these nonprofits represent a staggering $2.6 trillion in assets (see "Nonprofit Treasure Hunt" table for geographic concentrations of these assets). If you're looking for a public charity that can afford to pay a more competitive salary, you should think big: Large organizations with total assets of $10 million or more represent only 1.8 percent of public charities, but represent more than 92 percent of all assets held by public charities and take in 84 percent of all funds grossed by public charities. Also, keep in mind that a disproportionate share of nonprofit assets is concentrated in education and health organizations, particularly universities and hospitals.

Rank	State	Assets ($B)	Share of Total (%)
	Nonprofit Assets by State, 1995–2004		
1	California	636.4	24.3
2	Illinois	317.5	12.1
3	Minnesota	173.4	6.6
4	New York	150.3	5.7
5	Tennessee	137.9	5.3
6	Massachusetts	128.2	4.9
7	Georgia	101.7	3.9
8	Pennsylvania	96.4	3.7
9	Texas	75.5	2.9
10	Ohio	72.9	2.8
Source: National Center for Charitable Statistics (NCCS).			

All too often in nonprofits and professional services firms (with the notable exception of market research and business consulting firms), marketers find themselves misplaced and misunderstood. Even in larger nonprofit organizations with more funds for major campaigns, most positions calling on marketing skills are found in development and communications departments rather than an actual marketing department. In all except for the most entrepreneurial nonprofits, professionals with marketing skills spend far more time on fundraising campaigns, planning benefit events, and writing grants and reports than they do on projects that even remotely resemble for-profit marketing, such as developing effective fee-for-service campaigns. In professional services firms, many marketing positions are filed under sales and new business development—and unless the firm has a sound grasp on CRM and intangibles like reputation management and branding, marketers may find their efforts are judged almost solely by sales.

Professional Services

In many for-profit companies and services firms, you should be prepared to spend a significant amount of your time explaining your marketing methodologies, using market research findings to shape service and product offerings, setting reasonable expectations for ROI, getting top management buy-in for marketing strategies, and translating marketing results into terms everyone can understand. You should expect that after you've spent a few years in the field, few people in most services firms and nonprofit organizations will have your intuitive grasp of marketing metrics, jargon, research methods, trends, and industry-standard strategies. Unless you bridge the knowledge gap and let people in on your marketing thought processes, your career success may be limited—don't expect to be appropriately rewarded for your contributions until those around you fully understand why they are so valuable.

By Company

Industrywide generalizations often fail when it comes to specific companies. Take for example major toymakers; they're consumer goods companies, but not all of them are conservative. Your best cue about the culture of a company's marketing department may not be its industry segment or market position, but rather its physical layout.

For example, the marketing department at one prominent toy company has the run of an entire floor, laid out in sunburst formation around a central area with couches and toys. This company is an industry leader with strong core brands established through a willingness to take creative risks; it values the marketing department for the reputational and bottom-line benefits it provides. Marketers' jobs don't end when they leave the offices; they are charged with seeking the next big idea even in grocery stores and at the movies, and embodying their company's core values at all times.

Another toy company sandwiches its marketing department between R&D and sales in a cubicle maze on the floor of a former factory, with glassed-in conference rooms and toy displays around the perimeter. This company is an up-and-comer that emphasizes analysis and cross-functional teamwork to identify market opportunities and swiftly correct market miscalculations. Marketers are judged and rewarded strictly by the numbers. "It's high-pressure, but at least it's fair," says an insider. Marketers work long hours, often 12-hour days—but once they're home, they're off-duty.

Workplace Diversity

Again, broad characterizations often fail when it comes to describing workplace diversity in marketing departments across industries and companies. Nonprofits tend to be the most diverse working environments for marketers, and women often find themselves in the numerical majority. In stark contrast, upper management in marketing at consumer packaged goods and financial services companies is often characterized with the expressions "lily-white" and "old boy's club"—but then again, the same was said about technology marketing until a few years ago. This shift is not necessarily progressive thinking at work; it's often a matter of demographics. Companies across the industry spectrum have taken notice of census data showing the growth of "minority" populations in the United States into an aggregate majority, and are making a more concerted effort to hire marketers with expertise in these critical consumer segments.

Changing Markets, Changing Marketers

As these majority-minority markets continue to grow, so does interest in expertise on these markets. Competition among hospitals and professional services firms is heating up as they seek to diversify their client base with targeted marketing efforts in specific communities. Consumer goods companies are beginning to follow Ikea's lead and are seeking to capture the gay and lesbian market. U.S.-based companies like Starbucks seeking to cement a market leadership position both domestically and internationally are tasked with appealing to dominant "ethnic" markets at home and abroad. Bilingual and bicultural marketers—who have long been valuable assets to global category leaders like Coke and Pepsi—are finding that their talents are sought after in

> **As far as diversity goes, marketing is one step ahead of many other business disciplines in terms of actually seeking out candidates who relate to their markets.**

the U.S. marketplace as well as overseas. "As far as diversity goes, market-ing is one step ahead of many other business disciplines in terms of actually seeking out candidates who relate to their markets," says one African-American insider.

However, be advised that your gender, ethnic background, or sexual orientation are not sufficient qualities in themselves to qualify you as a marketing expert on the subject of women, ethnic consumer segments, or marketing to the gay and lesbian community. If you plan to position yourself as an expert in these areas, you'll need to do your research, build your portfolio, and manage your career accordingly. "Marketers who think they've got the inside track on the Hispanic market just because they were born in Mexico and speak fluent Spanish have another think coming," says one VP of marketing for a major Hispanic entertainment concern. "When I'm hiring, I look for more than bilingual skills. I want people who can prove to me they have the analytical acumen and creative capacity it takes to wrap your head around an extremely complex and increasingly influential market."

Opportunities for Women

Of course, don't expect marketer demographics to match marketplace demographics any time soon. Women have been a numerically dominant minority in many parts of the world for some time, yet even CPG companies that target women consumers and boast better hire rates for women than other industries are often short on female marketing directors and VPs. According to a recent survey from *Advertising Age*, men get paid more than women in equivalent positions across almost all management functions at advertising agencies, and men outnumber women almost three to one in top management positions. This survey reports that bigger firms aren't always necessarily more equitable with pay, either. On the contrary, women tend to get paid salaries closer to those of their male counterparts in agencies with an annual gross income of under $7.5 million.

However, the news is not all bad. *Advertising Age* reports that women have narrowed the pay gap in some seven of 11 advertising agency positions in 2002 (11th annual *Advertising Age* Salary Survey, 2003). Women are making inroads into the upper ranks at CPG firms as well, and female brand managers and marketing directors are holding companies to their reputations as being family-oriented by seeking and securing flexible job-share positions. Female marketers also have an established presence in health care and nonprofits and are making a small but noteworthy showing in the traditionally male-dominated (and more lucrative) fields of technology and financial services.

The entrance of talented female marketers in previously male-dominated fields has made these fields more competitive overall—which is good news for talented marketers both male and female, who now stand more of a chance of being recognized on the basis of their individual merits. Men in historically male-dominated industries can no longer count their gender as an advantage—but by the same token, women who used to be big fish in a small pond by virtue of their gender are finding that this is no longer a significant differentiator. "When I entered the tech field 10 years ago, you could count the number of women execs on one hand," says one pioneering female marketing VP. "Now I'm no longer quite the curiosity I once was. I know others who liked that added attention—but personally, I find it a relief to put that behind." On a more level marketing playing field, expertise becomes the prime mover—for everyone.

Compensation

Compensation for marketing positions ranges wildly according to industry, size of company, years of experience, and responsibilities. Some recent survey findings follow. The lowest-paid positions tend to be in the creative field, with many entry- to midlevel positions falling at or below $35,000. Marketing assistants typically fare better, earning starting salaries comparable to those of more experienced, specialized creatives. Market researchers have the most opportunities to move rapidly up the pay scale; they can break into the $40,000 to $60,000 range with as little as 2 years of experience to their credit. Salaries for Web-assisted market research and Web development positions aren't as attractive as they were just a few years ago, but they still fall at the high end of the salary spectrum for the market research and creative fields. Plus, positions requiring skills with new media are still relatively easy to enter with just a couple years of experience.

For experienced marketers, salaries often fall into the $50,000 to $80,000 range. Market researchers can reach $70,000 in just 5 years, while their counterparts on the creative side and in marketing and fund management are still in the $50,000 to $60,000 range. Salaries for marketing managers in nonprofit aren't always shabby, and some are even competitive with those of their peers at advertising agencies and companies. But at the marketing management level, services marketers with a handle on customer relationship management command the highest pay. At the senior executive level, the salaries for nonprofit marketers and principals of advertising agencies fall far short of salaries for marketers at professional service firms and CPG companies, particularly larger companies with multiple brands and millions in annual revenues.

Marketing and Market Research Salaries

Position	Salary ($)
Marketing Assistants	
Marketing/communications coordinator	27,500–39,250
Marketing assistant	34,219–38,749
Market Research	
Marketing researcher (entry level; 1–3 years' experience)	28,750–44,000
Web surfer/researcher	33,605
Level 1 market research analyst (0–2 years' experience)	44,276
Level 2 market research analyst (2–4 years' experience)	48,788
Level 3 market research analyst (4–6 years' experience)	64,436
Web/new media data warehouse specialist (2 years' experience)	67,820
CRM business data analyst (min. 6 years' experience)	78,414
Level 4 market research analyst (6–8 years' experience)	81,009
Web/new media data warehouse manager	91,823
Marketing Management	
Chief of direct marketing, not-for-profit	52,812[a]
Development director, not-for-profit	55,807[a]
Major gifts officer, not-for-profit	56,850[a]
Planned giving officer, not-for-profit	62,019[a]
Art director, advertising (min. 5 years' experience)	63,751
Marketing manager (min. 7 years' marketing experience)	69,248[a]
Marketing/new business manager	75,000[b]
CRM application administrator (min. 6 years' experience)	79,118
Product/brand manager (min. 4 years' experience)	80,240
CRM targeted marketing campaign manager (min. 8 years' experience)	102,815

Note: Median base salary, unless otherwise note. [a]Mean projected salary; [b]Median salary; [c]Plus bonuses and equity that may boost salary by as much as 50 percent at smaller companies, and 100 percent at midsized companies with lower base salary; [d]Plus compensation packages worth as much as $650,000 in stock and bonuses.

Marketing and Market Research Salaries (cont'd)	
Position	**Salary ($)**
Marketing Executives	
Fundraising/development director, not-for-profit (7 years' experience)	70,766
Agency owner/partner/principal	85,000
Marketing director, for-profit (min. 10 years' experience)	126,531
Top marketing executive, for-profit (min. 15 years' experience)	174,825
Senior VP in charge of single or multiple brands (at companies of $10 million-plus)	125,000 and 350,000[c]
Chief marketing officer (at large, multibrand company)	375,000–500,000[d]

Note: Median base salary, unless otherwise note. [a]Mean projected salary; [b]Median salary; [c]Plus bonuses and equity that may boost salary by as much as 50 percent at smaller companies, and 100 percent at midsized companies with lower base salary; [d]Plus compensation packages worth as much as $650,000 in stock and bonuses.

Sources: The Creative Group: 2004 Salary Survey; July 2004 data at www.marketingjobs.com. NonProfit Times 2003 Salary Survey; AIGA/Aquent Survey of Design Salaries 2004.

Benefits

Compensation is not the strongest motivator for most marketers, especially those in nonprofits. "Go into banking or consulting if you want to make money," says one insider. However, marketing does offer room for salary growth, as well as sizeable performance bonuses for high-performing marketers at profitable companies, and occasionally (though the practice is less prevalent now than a few years ago) employee stock options that accrue and vest the longer you stay with a company. A number of companies and larger nonprofits offer 401(k) plans, many with matching employer contributions. Individual consultants aren't so lucky—and unlike full-time marketers in organizations, they have to pay for their own health, vision, and dental benefits, too. Larger (or especially employee-centered) for-profit companies may offer butions, an employee cafeteria with discounted meals prepared by chefs, and health clubs on the premises.

Perks

As a marketer, you will have more opportunities than you might actually want to sample the product you are selling and others similar to it—but there are other freebies as well. "Ad agencies often treat their corporate clients to fine dining at expensive restaurants," says one well-fed marketer. "And of course if you're at an agency, you're expected to take out major marketing clients to meals. Either way you're eating well." Factor in the occasional lavish gift basket from an appreciative vendor, and you may need to make use of that employee health club.

Nonprofit marketers do not fare so well in the freebie department: One nonprofit fund development manager recalls after the first Gulf War in 1991, the U.S. army gifted her organization with more powdered government cheese than they could possibly use. "I think we probably still have some in our storage closet," she says.

Most important, marketing offers a tremendous opportunity to learn the fundamentals of business management on the job and hone a broad range of creative and analytical skills. For these reasons, marketing is excellent training for would-be executives and entrepreneurs, and a key point of entry and departure for many specialized fields. "If you want to build business that you can grow and influence, and learn how to build a company from the ground up, then marketing is the place to be," says one insider.

Vacation

Vacation is typically 2 to 3 weeks a year for most corporate, agency, and consulting firm positions. You may be expected to schedule your salary around seasonal swings in product cycles. For example, food and beverage marketers assigned to the Sprite and 7-Up brands should know that competition tends to heat up among lemon/lime carbonated beverages around the winter holidays and plan their time off accordingly. "There is a moderate amount of travel involved in most marketing jobs, and usually you can swing some vacation time around that," says one insider. Nonprofit marketers may have a little more leeway, since many nonprofit organizations offer comp time as partial recompense for the long hours generally logged by dedicated nonprofit staff. Independent consultants are the exception to the 2-week vacation rule—depending on the success of their business, they may get no vacation at all, or far more than they need.

Career Opportunities

Entry Level

MBAs have never been a strict career requirement for entry-level marketers. With some work experience to your name and the right connections through colleagues, friends, alumni, or professional associations, you may be able to land a marketing department internship or entry-level marketing position that involves more than photocopying. Some firms actually prefer to hire from within rather than compete for talented MBAs who may or may not fit into their organizational culture. As for market research firms, undergraduates with degrees in marketing and coursework in statistics, mathematics, survey design, advertising, and psychology can land entry-level jobs at these firms, though advanced degrees and technical training may be requirements to move into management positions.

"Before you invest in your MBA, make up a target list of the firms where you'd like to work," says one marketer. "If they hire from within, you don't need an MBA." At a CPG company, you may be able to work your way from a brand assistant position up to assistant brand manager and eventually become a brand or even category manager. An internship in a reputable ad agency and work on a few important accounts will get you started as a creative specialist, and from an ad agency you can leap to the corporate side. As an entry-level nonprofit fundraiser, your successful efforts on annual fund drives and other "asks" may win you a job as a development coordinator soliciting major donors and corporate sponsorships, which can in turn lead to a development director position. At a service firm, you may be able to segue from the front lines of sales or client management into the marketing department, where your firsthand knowledge of the customer could prove helpful in CRM efforts.

MBAs

Do you need an MBA to get ahead in marketing? Not necessarily—but it can certainly pave the way. Chief marketing officers, vice presidents, and marketing directors at larger organizations are typically expected to have an MBA from a well-regarded school for marketing, such as Northwestern, Dartmouth (Tuck), University of Michigan, University of Pennsylvania (Wharton), Georgetown, Harvard, or Ohio State. Your MBA may be a shortcut to a position as an assistant brand manager or marketing manager, saving you a year or two of rock-bottom, entry-level drudgery at the photocopier (though it won't save you from long hours of number-crunching).

However, MBAs with little practical marketing experience should not expect to be courted by recruiters with signing bonuses as they were during the dot-com era. Since companies like Enron and WorldCom that made a practice of hiring hot MBAs have gone down in flames, MBAs don't have the luster they once had. Now that high-paying consulting and financial services firms are recruiting less heavily, ad agencies and nonprofits have become more appealing for MBAs. You'll need to demonstrate returns for your work: successful grant writing as a development director at a nonprofit, new clients added to the roster at a services firm, or successful brand launches or relaunches at a CPG firm or ad agency.

Midcareer Professionals

Since solid business expertise, ROI, and careful profit/loss management are critical to marketing practice in an unpredictable economy, business-savvy midcareer professionals have gained an edge in the marketplace for talent. Midcareer candidates with extensive experience within a particular industry—say, sports team management—may find their insider's insight gives them a boost over the competition for a marketing role within their industry niche. You may want to bolster your position with training in your marketing niche, says one savvy marketer: "If it's advertising, take an advertising management course. If it's logistics, you need a logistics management class to learn the language, processes, and typical management problems in that field."

If you're a business or nonprofit executive, you are more likely to have the senior-level professional connections that can help you land a marketing job. That said, midcareer candidates shouldn't expect to make a lateral move from an executive level in another discipline (say, sales) to an equivalent position in marketing. You will probably have to work your way up from entry-level positions alongside people much less experienced than you, and the going can be rough for those used to steady advancement. Marketers win promotions through consistently exceptional performance; they don't advance automatically via seniority.

There are other cultural differences to contend with as well. Midcareer professionals used to delegating nonstrategic tasks to subordinates may find the team-based structures and entrepreneurial orientation of marketing challenging. Marketers often earn less than successful sales reps or accountants—so when you hear the salaries on offer for marketing positions, you may think twice about making the switch. Midcareer professionals with a background in sales, customer relations, and supply chain management may have an easier time making the transition to marketing, which may require more unconventional creative thinking than finance or IT types are accustomed to and more analytical structure than designers or PR types are used to. Given the right balance of analytical skills and creative problem-solving abilities, an established industry niche and a well-placed connection, midcareer hires can find themselves well-equipped to make their mark in marketing.

Market Research

This is the market research dream sequence: A recent graduate with a keen sense of inquiry and a good grasp of statistics lands a market research analyst position. The starting pay is good, and with a few years of experience and some impressive skills with data sets and the latest research software, the researcher is moving up the pay and promotions ladder faster than the marketing assistants across the aisle.

Now cut to real life and a grit-your-teeth-and-bear it job market, where recent graduates have to compete with MBAs and PhDs in social psychology or other discipline requiring strong communication and analytical skills for limited opportunities and, at best, incremental pay increases. Entry-level marketers with a couple of years of experience may find they need to take classes or even go to graduate school just to get to that next level of responsibility and pay. As it is, jobs early on will entail a lot of drudge work including copying, proofreading, inputting data, and so on. It's a dog-eat-dog, PhD-eats-MBA-eats-recent-grad world out there, and market researchers need to polish their analytical and technical skills to a high shine just to keep their jobs—and then add a few extras to get the edge on the competition.

Insider Scoop

What Employees Really Like

Entry-Level Marketers: What are you waiting for?

Although some may advocate waiting out the economic slump in an MBA program and emerging to greater career prospects, seasoned marketers say this logic is as flawed as it is defeatist. "I don't think you necessarily need to be an MBA anymore to move into a strategic role," says one seasoned marketer. "Many firms prefer to promote from within their ranks. Sure, the pay may not be great to start, but it beats paying for business school and taking yourself off the market for those 2 years. That's a huge loss. You should do your research to find out if your target firm promotes internally before you make that investment in an MBA." One added benefit of not having business school loans is that you can offer to start at the lower end of the pay scale, on the condition that your reviews will be scheduled at 3- or 6-month intervals instead of annually. That way, in 2 years you could be making the same salary as someone just getting out of grad school—and your salary may continue to climb incrementally while theirs remains subject to yearly review. Others may have more schooling, but you can still be the smarter marketer.

Brand Managers: It's a numbers game.

Versatility is the key to a successful career as a brand manager. "Brand management is not about any one discipline—it's not all about advertising, profit/loss management, or volume forecasting," says one insider with several notable brands to his credit. "If anything, it's a numbers game. You have to constantly keep an eye on numbers, tracking, managing, and interpreting them to come up with approaches that make market sense. That's how you build a name for yourself as a brand manager—not with splashy campaigns, but with effective ones." Many managers fall into certain product or service category specializations as a result of their work assignments, but this is not always the best long-term strategy when it comes to keeping your career options open. If you can demonstrate greater breadth of experience with a range of goods, services, and operating environments, you'll have a much better chance landing that prime marketing director position at a credit union than a marketer who has been promoting razors for 10 solid years.

Creative Specialists: Know your niche.

Finding your place in the sun is all-important for creative types. One former commercial producer doubled his ad agency salary as a freelance creative specializing in credit sequences. According to him, "It takes two things to run a successful business as a creative: a niche that no one else wants, and a style that no one can imitate. If your work is distinctive enough, your work becomes its own best advertisement." Unusual skill sets can be a competitive asset, too. Let's say your background is in health care, you speak Cantonese and English, and you designed your own website; that's quite a market niche in the making. For example, you might consider offering your multilingual Web content development services to HMOs, nonprofits, and private elder-care concerns serving communities with a substantial elderly Chinese-American population. Or you might specialize in developing bilingual websites and e-mail newsletters for acupuncturists and other traditional Chinese medical practitioners. So before you offer your creative services to others, be sure to apply your creativity to your own career.

Marketing Directors: Set your boundaries.

Meetings are the blessing and curse of marketing directors. More often than not, you'll find yourself in meetings with the senior management of your company or organization, key vendors (including advertising agencies and market research firms), strategic partners, lawyers, and accountants. As the necessary link among all of these constituencies, you become indispensable to your organization—and very well networked, should you want to make a career change. But you need to stay ahead of your market to be successful, and all of these meetings can consume your working hours and have you struggling just to keep pace with basic tasks. "Of all the challenges you'll face as a marketing director, managing your time will be the toughest," says one insider. "You're constantly in meetings and team projects, and there's inefficiency built into that group dynamic. To accomplish organizational goals, you have to set boundaries early, and learn to absorb and prioritize the bombardment of demands on your time." To make the most of your meeting time, set clear meeting agendas and leave enough time to go over key marketing concepts. Not everyone you'll meet with speaks the language of marketing, and you'll save yourself time and allow others to save face if you walk everyone through the marketing logic behind your ideas at the outset, before anyone has to ask.

Market Researchers: Use your head.

If you've got a head for statistics, you might just get ahead in market research. "A basic marketing research class will give you an overview of the process, but you will also need training in advanced statistical methods, including measurement design," says one expert researcher. "You will also want to take some classes in qualitative research skills, including focus group management and interpretation. And don't neglect operations research (OR) either. Modeling buyer behavior is increasingly important in data-driven marketing strategies, and making sense of that data requires some serious OR skills."

But don't expect to advance on data-crunching alone; you'll need communication skills and a certain sensitivity to your subject to help top execs and clients grasp and interpret your findings. "In a tough economy, market researchers are often the bearers of bad news," says one insider who specializes in the volatile consumer technology field. "You have to be more careful than ever about how you present your findings. Do it gently and constructively, so that no one is tempted to shoot the messenger."

Marketing Consultants: Observe the 40/60 rule.

Though independent consultants typically work long hours, they often do not get 40 billable hours in a week's work. "I go by the 40/60 rule," says one insider. "When I get a week where I'm able to bill out 60 percent of my working hours, that's a good week. With a week where I'm spending 60 percent or more of my time on nonbillable tasks like accounting, marketing my business, dealing with vendors, and responding to inquiries, that's a bad week."

Even with all of your responsibilities, consultants say, you need to be sure to carve out some downtime to keep your ideas fresh and in tune with the market. "Inevitably, some of your best ideas will come to you in the checkout line at the supermarket, when you see what's in the basket of the person in front of you, when you overhear what that kid is begging his mother for, or as you're flipping through some glossy mass-market magazine," says an insider. "So make sure you step away from your desk and get out in public at least once a day."

Watch Out!

Entry-Level Marketers: Overworked and underpaid.

This is not a job you'll want to keep forever. The data gathering and analysis can be tedious and strenuous, and the constant barrage of seemingly nonmarketing requests to check budget figures, run reports, take notes, get quotes from vendors, and order food for meetings will eventually wear you down after a couple of years. But if you rise above the tedium, you might actually learn something. Consider it on-the-job training about consumer behavior, vendor management, various promotional tactics, and products (or services) in your industry or within your brand's category.

Brand/Product Managers: Don't go down in flames.

If this position sounds like trial by fire, that's because it is. Companies regularly pull the plug on brands that fail to hit the all-important top-two or -three positions. The turnover rate is high, and it's common practice for companies to reassign brand managers to new brands every couple of years. "Burnout is a real issue," says one insider. If you want to stay marketable, you can't afford to be too myopic or fixated on the immediate tasks at hand. Notice what excites you most in your work, and clear out some time to cultivate those interests every day—even if it's only for 10 minutes. If you're interested in product development, you might use this time to study product recalls, track emerging consumer trends in an unexplored area, and build closer ties with your manufacturing division. Make sure you're expanding your skill set to keep your daily tasks stimulating—and to keep your career options open.

Creative Specialists: Try not to be a softie.

CFOs and other analytically minded types are wise to creative credential inflation and consider creative disciplines "soft" skills—and in a soft economy, your "soft" skills may be among the first to be discounted and discarded. So whether you work as a consultant or at a company, nonprofit, or ad agency, you should find ways to quantify your success to prove your value. How much money did you save a company by converting the promotional company newsletter from print to e-mail? How many corporate sponsorship dollars did your nonprofit client rake in as a result of your targeted corporate sponsorship campaign? How many users clicked through the Web banner you designed? If you don't want your number to be up just yet, make sure you have these numbers handy.

Marketing Directors: With great power comes greater responsibility.

Once you've landed this job, you'll finally be in a position to make decisions about your organization's overall marketing strategy. This may not always be so comfortable—when brands or service offerings under-perform, it will be your job to turn them around or to cut them to make way for more promising ones. And yes, cutting brands and services may mean cutting jobs. If you've ever wondered why there's a pay jump between marketing or brand manager and marketing director, you won't be wondering when you have to personally hand a pink slip to a longtime colleague. This is the moment when many aspiring senior executives discover that the added personal accountability for keeping ROI high isn't worth the extra pay. Others find that some time after personally breaking the news and seeing to it that departing employees are treated with all due dignity and respect, they are able to get some sleep at night. This is an individual choice every marketing director must be prepared to make—and remember, there's no shame in opting out of the marketing executive fast track at any point.

Market Researchers: Speak up; they can't quite hear you.

Don't think that because you spend a fair amount of your time dealing with numbers that you can hide behind them, and let them do the talking for you. You'll need strong communication skills to explain your research findings in accessible terms and to collaborate with other marketing team members on strategy and with IT on tracking tools. You'll also need to be able to communicate with your research subjects in their terms and often on their turf, whether in focus groups, in-home research, or on-location taste tests.

Few of your marketing colleagues get to interact with customers as often as you will, and if you're doing your job right, you'll gain personal insight and firsthand experiences that will be truly eye opening. Fun facts are all well and good, but interactions with customers can give you a deeper understanding of human behavior.

Marketing Consultants: Know your vendors.

Clients expect independent marketing consultants to be a one-stop shop, so if you aren't prepared to write marketing copy or provide website development strategy, you'll need to know several first-rate vendors you can rely on as subcontractors. Occasionally, you may have to look beyond your comfort zone for new vendors to meet the demands of a particular project. While it may seem disloyal to seek out a different Web engineer for a particularly complex Web development project, it's better to find the right engineer for the job than to knowingly mismatch your client with a vendor you selected just because you're on friendly terms. Also, though you may be able to keep your own books or write your own contracts, you probably won't have the time. To find reliable professionals familiar with the needs of small businesses, get referrals from other consultants and from professional associations of which you're a member.

Getting Hired

- The Recruiting Process

- Requirements

- The Hidden Job Market

- Stealth Marketing Tips

- The Tailored Portfolio

- Interviewing Tips

- Getting Grilled

The Recruiting Process

If you're expecting marketing jobs to come looking for you via corporate and consulting firm recruiters, make this your new career search mantra: "Recruiters are not my knights in shining armor." Several industry segments report decreased on-campus recruiting activity, both at the undergraduate and graduate level. Companies that recruited on your campus in the past may cut it from this year's roster, either as a cost-savings measure or because they are getting enough qualified candidates without the added effort and expense. Executive recruiters report they have something of a glut of qualified candidates. In the wake of high-profile executive ethical scandals, some companies are taking hiring decisions in-house where they can more closely monitor background and reference checks. Banking, finance, ad agencies, and other organizations are increasingly waiting for ambitious marketers to approach them—so don't keep them waiting.

If you have lined up an interview with a recruiter, make sure to read and understand the interview techniques described in the sections that follow, and go in with a tailored portfolio (also following). If you don't have enough relevant experience to fill a portfolio, go in with a tailored resume instead. For this, again, you'll need to do your background research on your target company. "You should hit the library, read their annual report, and do a fairly thorough search of business periodicals over the past year so you know the firm's products, customers, problems, and trends in the firm's industry," says one insider. "You want to impress upon the interviewer that you can hit the ground running."

Don't spend too much time playing the second-guessing game, trying to anticipate the recruiter's questions. Experienced recruiters generally avoid pat, predictable questions like, "So what is your greatest weakness?" By all means, review a few marketing fundamentals if it makes you feel more confident—it couldn't hurt to be reminded of Maslow's hierarchy of needs, Borden's classic 4Ps of marketing (product, place, price, and promotion), the three Ps recently tacked onto this equation (people, process, and provision of customer service), and Hudson's intriguing rival formula of the 5 Is (ideas, interactions, information, imagination, and interruptions).

Instead of trying to know all of the answers going into the interview, go in knowing what it is you want to convey about yourself and your experience. "Calm down, know yourself and your abilities, and be yourself in the interview setting," says a professor of marketing who counsels students going through the recruiter wringer every year. "You need to be able to present your past experiences in life and work within a marketing context. An example: You've been a waiter in a restaurant. That's an excellent marketing work experience. You've had to learn personal selling techniques, customer satisfaction, how to manage peak-demand situations, on the job stress. You've also had direct experience in how customer satisfaction is managed in a service encounter, and understand the complexities of managing services in a dynamic situation. Can you translate these meaningful experiences into something that's going to light up your interviewer?" If you're a true marketer at heart, there can be only one answer to this question: Yes.

Requirements

What does it take to succeed in marketing? Three things:

1. **A good balance of right- and left-brain thinking**, with the analytical acumen necessary to collect and analyze market data and see opportunities and the creative capacity to seize these opportunities with an appealing, convincing campaign. Those with slightly stronger analytical skills might be better suited to market research, whereas more creative types might opt for careers translating ideas to advertising images and marketing copy.

2. **A strong curiosity about what makes people tick** and drives them to make purchasing decisions. If you enjoy snooping in people's refrigerators and asking probing questions, you will find you have ample opportunity to indulge those instincts as a marketer.

3. **An academic and work history that reflects the first two items.** A solid background in liberal arts or business administration with at least a few statistics courses will be an asset to budding marketers, while market researchers with a strong background in social sciences and statistical analysis will have the advantage for entry-level marketing analyst positions. For more advanced marketing positions, an MBA is often considered a key asset to demonstrate the analytical rigor, creative problem-solving abilities, and intellectual curiosity necessary in an effective marketing executive. In terms of work history, any experience you have working retail or in your target industry niche will help you, even if it was on the front lines of customer service or sales. (Employers value marketers who have front-line experience of customer needs and desires, and bring that understanding to

their work.) A marketing internship would be ideal experience for entry-level marketers, and interns may find that they are offered a job at the end of their stint—many (if not most) companies prefer to promote marketers from within rather than seek out marketing candidates.

When it comes to academic credentials, a bachelor's degree with some background in statistics and basic computer knowledge (word processing, e-mail, Web searches, and spreadsheets) is the only qualification generally considered essential (though it's not always a must in creative positions such as Web design or art direction). According to the BLS' 2003 Occupational Outlook Handbook, the following might help position you for a career in marketing:

- **Courses in economics or business**, including business law, finance, and business administration may prove beneficial, particularly for marketers entering the financial services field or considering working for a multinational corporation.

- **An MBA** with an emphasis on marketing may help establish your marketing expertise with certain employers—especially if you happen to have attended the same MBA program that they did. Not all firms hire people straight out of college, and some recruit exclusively at MBA programs.

- **A bachelor's degree in engineering or science** in combination with some business courses can come in handy for marketers entering technical fields such as software or pharmaceuticals.

- **A bachelor's degree in advertising or journalism** may be highly regarded for CPG marketing roles and other marketing positions that require considerable creativity and unconventional thinking.

- **Coursework in social science research methods and mathematics** will prove helpful to marketers and market researchers alike, especially if these courses specifically address consumer behavior, market research and metrics, research methods, technology, and visual communication.

- **Foreign language abilities and experience living and working in another culture** will open up overseas job options considerably, as well as in U.S. companies with diverse target audiences.

- **Management training opportunities** should be seized, since advancement at a company may be contingent upon successful completion of such a program— and in any case, it looks great on a marketing resume. Take advantage of continuing education opportunities inside the firm where you're working or interning, and ask about tuition reimbursements for related coursework at local universities.

- **Certification, accreditation, and other professional marketing distinctions** are not common among marketers, so these are ways for you to set yourself apart from the pack and demonstrate your expertise. Consider signing up for

  - Sales and Marketing Executives International's management certification program.

  - IABC, The International Association of Business Communicators, which offers accreditation for marketing and communications professionals and awards the annual Gold Quill Awards for outstanding marketing programs.

  - The American Marketing Association's interest groups of marketers who specialize in a particular niche, such as nonprofit marketing or e-commerce.

The Hidden Job Market

If you're hoping to land your dream marketing job through a headhunter or a chance sighting of a job posting in the paper, you may have to keep dreaming of that job for a long, long time. The most prime marketing positions never make it to print or onto an executive recruiter's radar. News of them first spreads by word of mouth, sometimes even before positions are available.

When a new position has been inserted into a proposed departmental budget or a company is in growth mode, marketing execs often begin taking lunches with confidantes and put out feelers for potential candidates. When they hear a rumor that a position is about to be vacated (due to promotions, employees moving on, or poor employee performance), marketing execs get on the phone and start calling around to see who's available. "Never forget where anyone works, and never let them lose track of you, either," says one insider with several prime marketing gigs at Fortune 1000 companies to his credit. "Every job I've ever had I've gotten through the back door, through personal introductions."

By the time the position is officially announced, marketing execs have probably already corralled a couple of promising contenders. But before they unofficially close the applicant pool, they often circulate job postings through personal e-mails, postings on private listservs or professional or alumni association e-mail bulletins. These second-tier recipients enjoy the advantage of having some personal connection, however tangential, at the hiring organization, and may be able to follow up with that person for details or an informational interview. They usually hear of the opening well before it is announced in business publications, career websites, or classified ads. Even if they do not apply before the general public becomes aware of the opening, these applicants may save their applications from the slush pile by mentioning a respected source in the subject line of an e-mail (i.e., "Re: Tuck alumni newsletter posting") or the opening paragraph of the cover letter.

By the time this marketing job posting hits the open market and is culled by headhunters, it is almost certainly long gone. Organizations may be legally obligated to post job openings, but they're not legally obligated to consider your resume. Marketers build reputations for a living; if no one on the marketing team at the hiring organization knows the first thing about your personal or professional reputation, why should they entrust you with the reputation they've so carefully crafted for their brand or organization?

You need to make sure your reputation precedes you. The best thing you can do is to avoid wading through postings or taking resume workshops, and to network instead. Join your local alumni group, volunteer your time at a charitable organization, sign up for some listservs in your marketing niche, start attending parties you're invited to, pay your dues to your local AMA chapter organizations or other professional organizations. Suddenly you've made connections. Once you have some connections, start inviting them to lunch. It's cheaper than a resume doctor, more pleasant than hunting for elusive postings, and far more effective in tapping the hidden job market.

If you're shy about networking, here's a factoid that might get you over any initial discomfort: According to a survey initiated by The Creative Group, 48 percent of survey respondents are networking more than they were 3 years ago, with 21 percent reporting they are doing "significantly more" networking now.

In other words, if you want to compete in today's job market, networking is no longer even optional; it's a basic requirement to even make it past the 52nd percentile in the applicant pool. Think of it this way: If you wouldn't settle for a failing grade on an important school test, why would you accept it on one of the most important tests of your career? Do whatever you have to do to get over your shyness: Role-play an informational interview with a colleague, host a mock-networking party with friends, or take a public speaking class. If you're already networking, bravo. Now you're in position to enter the ranks of above-average candidates by scheduling that one extra lunch or meeting over coffee every other week.

Check out WetFeet's Insider Guide to networking—*Networking Works!*—for more practical advice on networking for career success.

Stealth Marketing Tips

The New Power Lunch

Marketers have a word for the most productive hour of their day: lunch. Ask a marketing colleague to lunch, and you'll soon learn that lunch is more important than any single job interview.

Here's why. Marketing is about relationships: among buyers and sellers, consumers and products, researchers and subjects, agencies and companies, consultants and clients. Before they'll entrust you with their marketing programs, employers want to know that you have a deep, intuitive grasp of relationships. That's what lunch is all about. By the time the bill comes (which you should be prepared to pick up, if you did the inviting), your strengths at building, understanding, and cultivating relationships should be abundantly clear.

If this kind of working lunch sounds somehow distasteful or like too much work, don't just shrug it off and decide a plan B will work just as well. As described in *Networking Works!*, this kind of networking is far easier than you might expect, frequently fun, and your best bet to getting the inside track on a great job that will be snapped up long before it's ever advertised (if indeed it ever is).

The Exponential Power of Lunch

Lunch is important, but it shouldn't be hard. You eat, you chat, you forge a bond with the person sitting across the table from you. Let's say you discover your mutual love of opera and Italian cuisine. Then, a few weeks or months later, you get the call:

- **It's your dining partner**. Word has it that there's about to be an opening on the marketing team, and they're right in the middle of a pasta brand repositioning. Officially, they'll still have to post the job once it becomes available—but unofficially, they'd rather not wade through all of those resumes. One month later: You've landed the job along with an attractive salary—you knew they needed a competent marketer fast, and they didn't want to play hardball and lose you.

- **It's a friend of your dining partner**, who mentioned you might be available for a consulting project. This friend needs someone to fill a vacancy on the Campbell's Soup new product marketing team short-term, just until they're able to find a new hire. Two months later: You are the new hire.

- **It's a friend of a friend of your dining partner**, who works at a major consulting firm pitching Charles Schwab and heard you used to work there. Would you be willing to consult on the project? Three months later: You're the new firm's in-house marketing guru on the financial services industry.

None of these opportunities would have come your way without lunch, and any one of them would be well worth the price of some sandwiches. But that investment gets even better: Over time, a single lunch could result in all three of these opportunities and more, as each opportunity branches into other opportunities. Marketers have a name for this, too: viral marketing.

Sure Beats Interviews

Compare lunch to your average job interview: a formal, high-pressure scenario where eating, chatting, and bonding are generally frowned on and relationship-building is virtually impossible. Your interviewer's goal is to fill a vacancy as efficiently and effectively as possible and return to the marketing tasks at hand. Now is not the time to engage an interviewer at length about opera—that would be a waste of time for the interviewer, for the company, and for you, too. So by the time you shake hands and walk away, the interviewer will have only the foggiest idea of who you are and what you are capable of, and the overwhelming odds are that you have no compelling personal reason to ever make contact again.

Lunch Before You Leap

If you've been invited for an interview on the strength of your resume alone or are interviewing with a recruiter, find a friend or a friend of a friend who works at that company and invite that person to lunch. By the time you go in for the interview, you may be equipped with insider insights about the company, their projects, and your interviewer that could help you turn a formulaic grilling session into a worthwhile conversation. Your new ally might even put in a good word on your behalf.

Mind Your Manners

Here are some tips for how to handle your lunch with grace and savvy.

DO

Eat. It gives your dining partner insight into your personality (you are what you eat, after all) and gives you something to talk about if the conversation lags. If you don't eat, you risk appearing tense and making the other person self-conscious.

Be forthright about why you wanted to meet. Don't leave your dining partner in suspense, wondering about your motives; broach the subject before dessert. Example: "I've been in financial services marketing for awhile—I've been working for Charles Schwab for 5 years—but I'm also a foodie, which has gotten me thinking about making the leap into food and beverage. Our mutual friend Carlos tells me you made a big switch from health care to F&B yourself. How did you pull that off?" If you're planning to apply for a specific position, say so—your dining partner may be able to advise you about how to get your resume noticed.

Cover interests besides work. Personal anecdotes and shared interests make for a deeper connection (and a more palatable lunch) than straight shoptalk. When it comes to hiring decisions or referrals, that connection can mean the difference between having a casual contact who dimly recalls you and having an enthusiastic advocate on your side.

DON'T

Be rude to the wait staff. Most people know better than to show up late for a first meeting—but if you are unavoidably detained, whatever you do, don't take it out on your server. In a 2003 survey initiated by The Creative Group, the majority of 250 respondents—which included 125 advertising executives from the nation's 1,000 largest advertising agencies, and 125 senior marketing executives from the 1,000 largest U.S. companies—named "being rude to wait staff" as the number-one mistake most likely to "hurt an advertising or marketing professional's chances of impressing a current or potential client during a lunch meeting." This error in judgment ranked considerably higher than any other mistake, including arriving late. Rudeness shows you lack the people skills needed to be a real team player, and the empathy required to intimately understand your customer base—plus you never know who used to wait tables, or whose best friend or close relative is a server. Select a lunch place where you know the service is reliable and you won't have any hassles. Even if the service is tortoise-slow, and you're running late for your next appointment, avoid finger-snapping at all costs and any sentence that ends with ". . . and make it quick!"

Pry. Due to confidentiality clauses and personal loyalties, your dining partner may not be able to give you a whole lot of specifics about a particular project or company. Try posing open-ended questions that prompt your lunch partner to divulge freely, rather than asking lots of probing, specific questions about profitability, performance issues, product plans, and the like. You don't want to be perceived as a corporate spy. If your dining partner seems uncomfortable with a subject, steer the conversation to a topic both of you can talk about comfortably. Your dining partner will appreciate your understanding, and leave lunch with a more positive impression of you.

Plead. It's never pretty, and it's especially unbecoming conduct for a marketer. It's not the customer's job to buy what you have to offer; it's your job to sell it to them. This is true in the labor market as well as in the market for goods and services. Your dining partner's respect is worth much more than his pity. You may get a referral or interview out of sympathy, but don't expect that contact to go to bat for you. Impress someone with your talents instead, and those referrals and recommendations will keep coming.

Play the joker. Follow quips with thoughtful insights to show you're not just a smart aleck. It's better not to wisecrack at anyone's expense, even at competitors of your prospective employer. Marketing is a collaborative field, and snide remarks and one-upmanship aren't welcome in it. Bear in mind that brand assignments are rotated every couple of years and client accounts get shuffled around frequently—so you never know where your interviewers used to work or consult.

The Tailored Portfolio

You've made it past lunch and onto the formal interview stage; it's the night before the interview. Like most ambitious marketers, you

1. Pick out an appropriate interview outfit, making sure it's clean, pressed, and presentable.

2. Print out multiple copies of your resume on nice paper stock.

3. Add a tear sheet from a recent print campaign to your portfolio.

4. Go over your background research on the company, and look over the bios of the entire marketing team for possible points of connection.

5. Role-play the interview with a partner.

6. Get a decent night's sleep.

7. Arrive at the interview promptly the next day.

Problem is, the above is inadequate preparation to distinguish yourself from all the other ambitious marketers who will doubtless be applying for the same position as you. If your contact at the organization has been pulling strings for you, you'd better be prepared to be extraordinary—or risk embarrassing your contact and thereby losing that all-important connection.

Let Your Portfolio Do the Talking

Can't you just talk your way into a job? Perhaps—but you'll have more respect going into the position if you let your accomplishments do most of your talking for you. Preparation and presentation skills are the hallmarks of any effective marketer, so walking in with a portfolio customized to make your case for this particular position shows you mean business. Tailor your portfolio to highlight

- Your expertise within the target organization's industry segment.
- Your expertise at performing the role that needs to be filled.
- Creative solutions to issues you know (from your background research and networking lunches) the organization is currently facing—slashed budgets, expansion into global markets, reputation management, brand extensions, and so on.
- Any come-from-behind marketing victories or instances in which expectations were exceeded.
- Successful campaigns your interviewer may have heard of or seen.

Intentional Omissions

You'll also need to weed out anything in your portfolio that doesn't directly support your case for your intended position, namely:

- Anything that looks or feels dated—you don't want to take valuable connection-building time explaining exactly how that tagline captured the zeitgeist of the late '80s.
- Anything from a company known for its unethical dealings, Chapter 11 flameouts, or spectacular disappointments—including most dot coms.
- Work from organizations where your performance was less than stellar (you don't want to run the risk that someone asks a contact there about your performance).
- A bulk of work from industries that are entirely unrelated to your target organization's niche, such as a pile of nonprofit educational brochures for a for-profit position marketing furniture.

Show and Tell

Once you have exactly what you need in your portfolio to make a strong case for the position on offer, you should practice walking someone through your portfolio. Effective storytelling plays an important role in selling products, services, and grant proposals, and it will help you sell your abilities. With each work sample, tell a succinct story of a problem encountered or opportunity discovered—and make sure it has a happy ending. Try not to linger too long on any one example/story, and give your role-play interviewer the opportunity to ask questions. Pull your interviewer in with questions and relevant personal insights, and give numbers to substantiate success wherever possible.

Storytelling Sample

Here's how this storytelling technique might work to explain a (fictional) shoe brand turnaround in an interview for a marketing position at a jeans manufacturer:

"You remember how big Xuma gym shoes were in the '70s, right? Well, the brand didn't exactly hold its own in the '80s and most of the '90s. When I was first assigned the brand at my consulting firm, I thought, 'Man, what did I do to deserve this?' But then I did some background research with coolhunters, and found that urban hip hoppers were digging the older styles of Xumas out of closets and thrift stores—they went from being just plain old to 'old school' cool. So we tested the waters by releasing a limited edition of an original design circa 1980. We sold out that edition in a month, outselling every new shoe release that year. The company took our recommendation to redefine the brand as 'old school,' and they tell me sales last year exceeded projections by 123 percent in the United States and by more than 200 percent in Italy and Japan."

Make Your Numbers Count

Big numbers may be initially impressive, but your audience will have a hard time remembering them later unless you present them in a context that is memorable and meaningful to your audience. Consider the difference between these statements:

"While I managed the annual fund drive, we made 100 percent of our campaign goal."

"The first year I worked on the annual fund drive, we were up against some serious odds to reach our goal of $180,000 to help build our new facility. This goal was twice the amount raised the previous year, so it was already pretty ambitious—especially in the middle of an economic slump, when donors are courted by many worthy nonprofits in dire straits. The development director position had been vacant for 4 months before I took the job, so we were starting from behind, too. Then tragically, the significant other of one of our longtime board members was diagnosed with cancer. So of course she had to step down, leaving some giant shoes to fill as the charismatic chair of the fund development committee. I put out some feelers for a replacement, and soon heard that a friend of a friend who'd recently finished an impressive term as the chair of the board of another nonprofit might be interested. I told him I needed a partner on the board who wasn't afraid of a challenge, and described my plans to reach out beyond the usual affluent donors to request modest donations from middle-income community members who responded to our survey last year. With his help training and inspiring board members to make fundraising pitches, support from corporate sponsors who provided in-kind gifts to donors of all levels, and a kickoff picnic event at the future site of our new facility, we made that $180,000—and we've met our goal every year since, too. But that year was special for me, because several board members made donations in the name of our former board member and her loved one.

Dedicating that plaque on our brand-new facility with her entire family present was a profoundly moving experience."

Stick to Your Story

If you don't have many stories to tell in your portfolio, don't despair; create a story around what you do have. Take your cue from this true story of an ambitious marketing student, who wanted to break into ad copywriting, but had little practical experience: He created a portfolio spoofing automobile ad campaigns, presenting himself as the hot new model. "His ads were creative, funny, and concise in presenting himself," says one marketer who saw the portfolio. "They were also incredibly well designed: He helped a design student prepare portfolio descriptions in exchange for design services. He was resourceful, talented, and managed to talk himself into a creative position at an ad agency in Chicago. He surprised me with his ability to land a job at a higher pay than he might have expected. He's since been hired away from that agency and is in New York now."

Interviewing Tips

When it comes time to market yourself in an interview, think about how you'd position a product for success in the marketplace. The same rules apply.

1. Examine your target audience, its needs, and opportunities.

2. Define how you will meet your audience's needs and opportunities and provide added value.

3. Outline an overall strategy to convey this message to your target audience.

4. Craft stories that will help sell key message points to your target audience.

5. Implement your plan.

6. Evaluate your success.

7. Solicit feedback to identify success factors and earmark areas for improvement.

That may sound like an undertaking, but as a marketer you know that it's your job to make it seem effortless. Here are some tips to help make your interview an engaging, winning campaign:

DO

Research, research, research. This means learning everything you can about the organization in question via personal contacts, Web research, television ads you've recorded, and collateral materials (e.g., annual reports, brochures, etc.)—but don't stop there. Study the organization's chief competitors and the industry in general. If you're interviewing with a market research firm, you'll need to familiarize yourself with any recent findings it has made public and the industries it covers. If you're interviewing with a CPG company, get to know that company's key brands intimately. Visit stores that carry them for insights about each key brand's four Ps (product, price, placement, and promotion) and three Cs (competition, company, and customer). If the organization is in the business of providing services (e.g., health care, hospitality, nonprofit), learn about the marketplace for those services and key differentiators. For high-tech and biotech, don't forget to bone up on the latest developments and the accompanying terminology as well as key offerings and competitors. If you know who's going to interview you, do some research on that person as well.

Role-play beforehand. Ask a marketing colleague (preferably in the same business your prospective employer is in) to present you with a series of personal questions and hypothetical marketing scenarios. Many candidates make the mistake of preparing for scenarios but not for personal questions, reasoning that they know themselves well enough to wing them. But as in marketing goods and services, marketing yourself to prospective employers means coming up with a few concrete messages you want to leave with your target audience, and identifying the stories and examples that will drive them home most effectively. Be sure your stories demonstrate your marketing core skills (leadership, teamwork, analytical skills, multitasking, creativity, people skills), but also highlight some unique qualities or experience that will differentiate you from the pack (experience with a major competitor or internationally recognized brand, noteworthy successes, niche market expertise). After you've finished your role-play, ask your "interviewer" what three messages you've conveyed. If what your interviewer recalls are not the messages you intended, you should adjust your answers accordingly.

Listen actively. When your interviewer presents you with a scenario, listen for what is really being asked of you. "How would you redesign this company's corporate identity?" may seem to be a question about your creative abilities, but the interviewer may be testing your strategic acumen (Is a redesign really warranted?), research skills (How do you evaluate brand identity?), or your ability to work creatively as part of a team (Who might bring fresh thinking to the table?). Be responsive and engaged, and turn questions around on your interviewer—for example, "What precipitated the need for a redesign?" Share your ideas and demonstrate that you know how to involve others in problem-solving, and you'll prove yourself a dynamic, creative team player.

DON'T

Brag. Selling yourself as "the best hire you'll ever make" prompts skepticism in the job market, just as a hyped-up claim about a product would in the consumer goods marketplace. State your case, but don't overstate it. Be specific about the expertise you bring to the table, rather than such generic, overblown attributes as a head for business or fancy footwork. Being smart doesn't cut it anymore—employers are looking for profitability and follow-through, not merely big ideas.

Hold a fire sale. Employers are looking for long-term value, not cheap goods, so don't sell yourself short just to get your foot in the door. Bargains give off the faint whiff of desperation, and that's never appealing to an employer, however thrifty. Plus, employers know that if they take you up on your once-in-a-lifetime offer, you may come to resent them for it later. Don't even bring up pay until you've established your worth to your prospective employer. They'll be far more impressed with a campaign you initiated that netted $2.5 million than a $20,000 cost savings on your salary. If you are willing to accept a pay cut from your current position or a starting salary at the lower end of the pay scale, you should make it conditional on a quarterly or semi-annual review during which your pay will be reassessed to more closely reflect the value you bring to the organization.

Fawn. Golly gee, you're just so honored to land an interview with such brilliant people. . . . That's all well and good, but check your urge to gush at the door. Collegial respect is a better building block for a solid creative partnership than a bundle of warm fuzzies. These are marketers you're talking to; they deal with schmoozing vendors and ad agency reps often enough that they can spot brown-nosing at 100 yards. Keep your dignity, and you just might land the job, too.

Getting Grilled

Your interview will probably include a variety of questions aimed at gauging your past and future performance, so you should come equipped with at least ten stories demonstrating what a great team asset you've been in the past, and what particular strengths and skills you might bring to the company. By now you should have researched the company inside (through your networking contacts) and out (from checking out stores, websites, advertising, publications, and events where the company's product is featured). This should give you a pretty good idea what the company wants to hear—so tailor your stories and interview responses to match. You should come prepared to handle each of the following types of questions, molding your response as best you can to highlight your strengths.

Behavioral Questions

Behavioral questions probe your past work behavior for an indication of what the company might expect from you. In answering these questions, you should remember not to go on telling some long-winded story your cousin found hilarious but doesn't really highlight your strengths. Cut to the chase, and use your story to highlight your leadership, teamwork, strengths, skills, and resourcefulness. Some examples:

- Please tell me about a time when you were part of a cross-functional team, and how you dealt with the range of skills and personalities around the table. Who did you find the most difficult to get along with? What about the easiest?

- Can you describe an instance when you had to juggle multiple brands at once? What challenges did this raise for you, and how did you handle them?

- Can you give me an example of a time when you took the initiative to seize a market opportunity? How did you identify this opportunity, and how did you marshal the resources necessary to act on it?

Hypothetical Questions

Hypothetical questions begin with "How would you . . ." or "Imagine if you were to . . ." or "What would you do if . . ." Your initiative, creativity, and ability to respond to the unknown are being tested here, so while you can repeat the question and ask clarifying questions to buy yourself time to come up with an answer, you do need to think fast to show how smart you can be under pressure. Think logically and reason through your answer, and your interviewers will still be impressed even if they don't get the exact answer they're looking for. Some examples:

- What would you do to get an ad agency that was 2 weeks late delivering creative to deliver quality work ASAP?

- If you suspected a piece of market research was faulty, what would you do about it?

- If you were a marketer at this company, what new product would you recommend we introduce to the market and why?

Case Questions

Case questions test your ability to analyze a problem or opportunity, perform under pressure, make use of appropriate resources, offer creative solutions, and sell your ideas to your interviewer. You'll be given a series of facts, variables, and resources, and be asked to come up with an appropriate solution on the fly. This exercise will test your creativity, but before you come up with an ingenious answer, be sure you're solving the right problem—case questions can be trick questions. Restate what you heard and ask clarifying questions to make sure you've got the problem right, then reason aloud through your answer. In your analysis, be sure to cover the 4Ps (product, price, placement, and promotion) and 3Cs (competition, company, and customer). If there's an equation involved, check your math twice. Then when you've come up with your solution, sell it to your interviewers as the best possible approach to cover all 4Ps and 3Cs, even if they're initially inclined to disagree with you. This is where your presentation skills and persuasive powers should come in handy. Remember, you're a marketer, so it's your job to sell to skeptics! (If you'd like more practice in this area, check out WetFeet's *Ace Your Case* series.)

You can expect case questions about

- Market sizing: For example, how many minivans are there in the United States?

- Business operations: For example, a reliable vendor in Japan has just doubled its price for the paper you use for your packaging. You could use a Canadian vendor, but there are issues with value-added tax and a secondary vendor upon whom they rely for paper pulp. What steps would you take to keep costs under control and keep the supply chain as streamlined as possible?

- Business strategy: Soda brand X has been one of the top two brands in the United States for decades, and now the company is considering launching a new and improved formula for the brand. What steps would you advise the company to take?

- Resume: I see that you used to work for a major financial services company. Suppose that your small business loan program isn't attracting many new customers in expanding Midwestern markets, even though your pricing terms are essentially the same as those of your competitors, whose new business account numbers skyrocketed last year. List options to improve the program without altering your pricing policies, and then prioritize those ideas according to their relative cost-effectiveness.

Generic Questions

Your interviewers probably have a lot else on their minds besides hiring you, so chances are they'll rely on a few stock questions to lighten their interviewing load. This is good news for you. These questions may seem terribly obvious, but that makes them the easiest to prepare for and mold to fit your strengths.

- Tell me about yourself.

- What appeals to you most about this position?

- Why did you leave your previous job(s)?

- What are your three greatest strengths and three greatest weaknesses?

- What's one problem you wish you had handled differently at your last job?

- How would you describe your management style?

- What special skills can you bring to a cross-functional team that already includes techies, researchers, and R&D specialists?

- Can you tell me about a marketing project or campaign you're particularly proud of? What about one you'd rather forget?

- Where do you see our company's Brand X heading in 3 years? What about the category as a whole?

- Where do you see yourself in 3 years, and how do you plan to get there?

- What kinds of people would you say you have the easiest time working with? What about the hardest?

- How do you usually handle pressure?

- What special insights can you bring to the table about Brand X's target audience?

- What do you think our company could learn to market Brand X more effectively from its competitors?

- Can you tell me about a time you learned the hard way how not to market a product or service?

- Tell me about a time when you took a leadership role on a project.

- What skills would you expect to hone further in this position?

- Why should I hire you?

For Your Reference

- Industry Jargon

- Books

- Publications

- Associations

- Other Online Resources

Industry Jargon

Adoption curve/process. Shows when consumers are most likely to become receptive to a marketing message. Trendsetters come first, early adopters follow, the early majority comes next, then come the cautious late majority, and in dead last are the laggards, who prefer to keep on doing things the way they always have.

To visualize how this works, think of how people have responded to home computers: First came Silicon Valley engineering types; then came scientifically inclined students and professors, and tech-savvy business people who increasingly relied on computers at work; then came the bulk of students and business people; later came the bulk of computer users, including business people who were reluctant to give up the word processors they'd invested in and students who'd previously used computer labs; and finally came the people still wedded to their 1939 Smith Corona typewriters but unable to find replacement typewriter ribbons for them.

AIDA. This model describes effective promotion as a four-step process:

1. Get the target consumer's **attention**.

2. Hold the target consumer's **interest**.

3. Arouse the target consumer's **desire**.

4. Obtain the target consumer's **action**.

Bait pricing. Using a low price to lure a customer into a store, then pushing more expensive brands to the customer inside the store. This is what's happening when you find that sale-priced MP3 player advertised in the paper sitting inconspicuously on the shelf right next to the new deluxe model with a placard announcing its many attractive features.

Bias for action. Marketers with a bias for action are inclined to swing into action on campaigns rather than pore over market research indefinitely—a habit known as *analysis paralysis*. Market researchers are tasked with looking at the market, but marketers must know when to stop looking and start leaping at market opportunities.

Brand extensions. New offerings that piggyback on the success of existing brands.

Brand insistence. What every marketer hopes her product will inspire in customers: such devotion to a product that the customer is willing to search for it if necessary.

Break-even analysis. Determines if and when the company will be able to cover its costs at a particular price, given various sales volumes. Market researchers should expect to get intimately familiar with this type of analysis.

Buy-in. You'll need to secure this from the executive team to get the funds to pursue extensive market research, new product ideas, brand extensions, and most other marketing ideas that occur to you besides. Beware micromanaging execs—selling your ideas to these decision-makers can take up more time than marketing to consumers, and cause you to miss market opportunities.

Cobranding. When two or more companies or entities team up to offer products or services that bear both of their brands simultaneously, such as Skippy and Smuckers teaming up to create a swirled peanut-butter-and-jelly spread or products carrying the Good Housekeeping Seal of Approval or Fair Trade Certified label.

Competitive advantage. The magic mix of marketing strengths and product attributes that allows a product to prevail over its competitors in the marketplace.

Cross-functional team. A marketing team at many companies consists not only of professionals with expertise in marketing and market research, but also technology, R&D, finance, and sales. Effective marketers can speak the lingo of all these disciplines and manage cross-functional teams.

Differentiation. Highlighting the unique characteristics of a brand to convince consumers to buy your product or service over comparable ones. This requires very careful positioning and a certain finesse in the financial services arena, where service offerings are often very similar due to legal standards and interest rates set by the government.

Direct marketing. The bread and butter of many marketers and the bane of many consumers' existence, this covers marketing appeals delivered directly to the consumer by means other than face-to-face selling: direct mail, telemarketing, and e-mail blasts (a.k.a. spam). "Opt-in" appeals targeted to consumers who sign up to receive such solicitations tend to yield a higher return on investment than mass direct marketing appeals.

Dumping. Selling a product overseas at a price below the cost of production in that country, either to offload domestic surplus or drive foreign competitors out of business. This practice is strictly forbidden under most trade agreements, but it still happens.

Early adopters. The consumers who follow the lead of trend instigators in adopting a marketing idea. This group usually consists of opinion leaders whose positive opinion can influence their peers to adopt the idea, resulting in early majority backing for a marketing concept.

EDLP and Hi/Lo. Retailers usually fall into one of two categories: "Every Day Low Price" stores offer low prices across the board, while "Hi/Lo" retailers periodically run deals and discounts on their premium products.

Equilibrium point. An economic dream come true, this is the point at which the quantity and price sellers are willing to offer is equal to the quantity and price buyers are willing to pay. Once this point is reached, there will be no seller surplus or unmet consumer demand.

Fishbone diagram. You may hope you'll never have to draw one of these, but there's probably no avoiding it. This is the sketch you make to dissect a marketing problem and find out where a promising marketing campaign went wrong. If there are only one or two decisions out of joint and you catch these early on, perhaps the campaign can be salvaged. Otherwise, it's a live-and-learn, sink-or-swim business world, and you'll probably have to either cut your losses or rebrand.

Flanker brands. Brands that protect the flanks of your flagship brand by covering a variety of alternative market niches and price points, and taking up shelf space to shut out competitors. Do keep in mind that you don't want to put your brands in direct competition with one another, though. When Gap Corp. launched the successful, lower-priced Old Navy and took the Gap upscale, its premium Banana Republic brand began to suffer. Flanker brands should complement, not compete.

Flexible pricing. This is when you sell the same products or services to different customers at different prices, as when premium items are sold at lower prices in developing overseas markets or branded goods sell at different prices at department stores, discount chain stores, and online. Proceed with caution, because this strategy can backfire: Selectively lower prices can cause a luxury brand to lose its cachet, and online discounts can drive customers away from stores that feature your entire product line. Flexible pricing is sometimes a matter of ethics and necessity in the pharmaceutical industry, which has been successfully pressured by governments and activists to lower prices for retroviral drugs in developing countries.

FMCG. Fast-moving consumer goods, including packaged foods or toiletries.

Focus group. A group of usually six to ten people (typically paid for their participation) who represent potential markets for your branded product or service whom you interview to tease out potential market opportunities and solicit feedback to your marketing ideas. This is qualitative research, and the ideas explored in them are often subject to further testing with quantitative studies such as surveys for their broad applicability to the market.

FSI. Free-standing inserts are the newspaper inserts that offer coupons and fill recycling bins across America. The average redemption on FSI coupons is only 2 percent, but they can drive sales on many brands and deliver a return rate twice as high as the most successful Web banner advertising.

GRPs. Gross rating points, which measure advertising impact.

Iceberg principle. According to this principle, key marketing information is often hidden in the summary data. This is market researchers' comeback to marketers who have a bias for action and are inclined to gloss over research findings in their hurry to initiate a campaign.

Ideate/ideation. Other ways to say "brainstorming."

Institutional advertising. Sales pitches focused on selling consumers on the organization and its reputation, rather than a specific product or service. Marketers often shy away from this promotional approach, since it's more difficult to show bottom-line impact of a campaign aimed at winning consumer admiration instead of consumer dollars—but sometimes it's necessary, especially when entering a marketplace or after a scandal.

Market maturity. The point at which sales for a particular product or service begin to level off, when a product or service is not so new any more and the going gets tough for any brand still in that market.

Market position. This assessment of a brand's strength is typically calculated by multiplying market share by mind share (both defined below).

Market segmentation. Identifies likely consumers for a particular product or service, and groups these consumers according to similar characteristics or behavior patterns. This process helps identify the right marketing mix to appeal to the target markets for a product or service.

Market share. What every marketer wants to gain, market share is your company's sales volume as a percentage of total sales volume for the market your company competes in.

Mind share. An attempt to quantify how likely consumers are to think of your company and brand, as opposed to those of your competitors.

Niche marketing. Marketing that is carefully targeted at a very specific demographic, such as 35- to 42-year-old stay-at-home soccer moms of preteen suburban girls whose family income is more than $100,000.

Nielsen and IRI. The research firms that track store sales, television viewership, and many other vital statistics for marketers. Nielsen and IRI sales database information is typically updated on a weekly or monthly basis as new scanner data is processed, while the famous Nielsen television ratings are available weekly so that marketers can adjust media buys (purchases of advertising time).

Nonprice competition. Using placement, packaging, or promotion to sell a product to consumers, instead of trying to win them over by offering a lower price than that of competitors. This may sound like pulling a rabbit out of a hat, but as a marketer you'll be expected to pull it off successfully as a matter of course.

Positioning. A catchall term that describes your efforts to make a brand seem unique in the marketplace and the most desirable choice among products or services in its category for your target market. Your positioning strategy will range from PR and advertising to product features, pricing, and packaging.

Psychographics. Also known as *lifestyle analysis* or *AIOs*, which stands for consumer activities, interests, and opinions. This is the kind of soft, often speculative social science that makes market researchers roll their eyes if not executed carefully and supported with actual data.

Push/pull. Push is the extent to which you drive consumer choices by advertising and other unsolicited promotions, as opposed to pull: the ways that you appeal to consumers to engage with you and entice them to register on your website, sign up for promotional newsletters and mailings, and participate in promotional events.

Qualitative market research. Exploratory research that poses open-ended questions to consumers to uncover market opportunities and provide insights about various possible product features and marketing approaches. Think focus groups and essay questions, not yes/no or multiple-choice surveys.

Quantitative market research. Structured research that seeks solid, generalizable answers to specific questions that can be expressed in numbers, ratios, averages, means, or percentages, such as, "91 percent of the survey sample of 5,000 ketchup consumers strongly preferred red ketchup to green ketchup, while 86 percent of the target group of 6- to 12-year-olds expressed a strong preference for green ketchup, and the average mother of 6- to 12-year-olds in our study indicated no strong preference for either red or green ketchup."

Reach versus frequency. The classic advertising tradeoff: Either you appeal to a broad audience a few times (think ads made specially for the Superbowl) or reach a few people very frequently (e.g., a banner ad in a daily legal brief e-mail newsletter aimed at intellectual property lawyers).

Rebranding. Revamping a brand after an earlier branding attempt fell short of expectations, the demographics of the market for the brand have shifted, or there's been some significant change in the brand.

Research proposal. A document outlining what kind of market information will be sought and the methods by which this data will be obtained.

Response rate. The number of people in a research sample who respond to a questionnaire or survey.

Return on investment. Ratio of after-tax profits to the investments made to gain that profit—including marketing expenses—times 100 to remove decimal points. Keep your attention focused on delivering a return on investment, not just high profits—you need to keep your costs under control even as you drive up profits.

Secondary data. Research that is already available on a specific topic. A smart market researcher knows that the first step in any market research is to find out what information is already available, saving time and money in data collection.

SKU (stock-keeping unit). Pronounced "skew," this is a number assigned to all CPGs. Each individual package size and/or product variety is considered a separate SKU, and you can track sales of your SKUs through research services like Nielsen and IRI.

Slotting. The price paid to the trade to "slot" your product into a space on the shelf, which is no small matter—slotting fees are still a significant cost of doing business for CPG companies.

The trade. In the CPG world, this is the slang term for the retailers and vendors who sell your products. These are the people you'll need to cozy up to if you want to ensure prime placement for your products.

Value added. What you should bring to your organization as a marketer, and what your product or service should deliver to the customer.

Volume. Sales volume, which is usually the first place execs look for marketing wins. It will be your job to redirect their attention to return on investment, so that they can see the potential in smaller brands that are doing well and hear your argument about why some of the capital dedicated to high-volume, low-return behemoth brands should be distributed to other brands.

Books

From WetFeet

The following WetFeet titles are all available online at www.WetFeet.com and www.Amazon.com. See the last 2 pages of this Insider Guide for a complete list of WetFeet Insider Guides.

Careers in Brand Management

Learn what it takes to break into the field of product marketing, who the key players are, what to expect from an interview, what the opportunities are at your level of experience and expertise, and where there's room for advancement.

Networking Works! The WetFeet Insider Guide to Networking

Find out how you can get the jump on those great jobs you hear about but never seem to see postings for, and what it takes to land them yourself, from the initial contact through all-important lunch meetings and follow-up.

Ace Your Interview! The WetFeet Insider Guide to Interviewing

Learn what employers are looking for and how to give it to them in an interview, from key preinterview research through interview prep for commonly asked questions and curve balls, through effective follow-up strategies.

Other Helpful Books for Budding Marketers

Will & Vision: How Latecomers Grow to Dominate Markets

Gerard J. Tellis, Peter N. Golder, and Clayton Christensen (McGraw-Hill Trade, 2001).
Winner of the American Marketing Association's Berry-AMA Book Prize, this book takes a longer view of marketing success and reveals that latecomers, not first-to-market companies, often hold market advantage.

Positioning: The Battle for Your Mind, 20th Anniversary Edition

Al Ries and Jack Trout (McGraw-Hill Trade, 2000).
This update to a classic text explains the key business and marketing strategies needed to lodge your product or service in the minds of customers, winning valuable mind share in the race against competitors

The End of Advertising as We Know It

Sergio Zyman and Armin Brott (Wiley, 2002).
Former Coca-Cola CEO Zyman contends that the reign of the television and radio spot is over, and sales must now be cinched by a complex marketing mix of branding, packaging, celebrity spokespeople, sponsorships, publicity, and customer service.

The Tipping Point: How Little Things Can Make a Big Difference

Malcolm Gladwell (Little, Brown, 2000).
A fascinating theory from the New Yorker columnist that describes how big ideas start small, and then catch on—key reading for any budding marketer.

Purple Cow: Transform Your Business by Being Remarkable

Seth Godin (Do You Zoom, Inc., 2002).
Learn how to make your mark and move up the ladder by looking past traditional marketing methods, and learning from market leaders like HBO, Starbucks, and JetBlue about how to build an extraordinary brand.

Publications

Brandweek (in print or online at www.brandweek.com)

Provides key industry statistics, including industry rankings, media expenditures, sales data, and category analysis as well as breaking news in brand management, background on culture trends (box office grosses, music sales, etc.), and coverage of current marketing trends. Premium content, such as Career Network Services and Superbrands "Top Brand" listings, is only available with a paid subscription.

Adweek (in print and online at www.adweek.com)

A sister publication to *Brandweek* (and owned by the same parent company as *Mediaweek* and *Technology Marketing*), *Adweek* offers breaking advertising industry news, creative coverage, and culture trend information. *Adweek* reports rankings of agencies by region and nationwide for the United States, rankings for interactive and direct response agencies, and listings of top online and magazine advertisers. Premium content (accessed only by paid subscription) includes Career Network Services, Premium Classifieds, Agency Report Cards, and Accounts in Review.

New York Times (www.nytimes.com/pages/business/media/index.html)

Covers Madison Avenue and other business and marketing trends in print and online. NYTimes.com offers free content and services of interest to marketers and job seekers, including free subscriptions to advertising columnist Stuart Elliott's *In Advertising* weekly e-newsletter at www.nytimes.com/mem/email.html. Regular *In Advertising* features include Campaign Spotlight, Q&A, Webdenda: People and Accounts of Note, and The Week in Advertising. For an overview of entry-level positions currently available in the field, use the Quick Search feature for marketing/advertising at www.nytimes.com/pages/jobs/index.html.

Associations

American Marketing Association (www.marketingpower.com)

The AMA's site offers an impressive range of guides, webcasts with marketing experts, and practical, informative articles free to nonmembers, offering substantial career tips and need-to-know marketing information on such subjects as CRM, target audience segmentation, and translating market research findings into business action plans. The AMA publishes *Marketing News*, a widely referenced publication covering the latest career and industry trends, and subscriptions available for free to members. Members can also elect to receive the AMA's *Marketing Matters*, an e-newsletter on the state of the industry.

Market Research Association (www.mra-net.org)

Most of the detailed job descriptions, career-building articles, salary links, and industry insights on the MRA's website are available to members only. MRA publishes *Alert!*, described as "a monthly magazine with 40 pages of information on the opinion and marketing research profession," and a membership roster called the Connector. These are free to members, or available for sale to nonmembers on the MRA website.

The Qualitative Research Consultants' Association (www.qrca.org)

For market researchers who can't get enough of dyads, triads, focus groups, and in-depth research, this is the association for you. Includes helpful definitions for key types of qualitative research specialties, and consultant listings around the country.

Other Online Resources

MarketingJobs.com

This site has current salary listings for a wide variety of job titles, cross-referenced with years of experience and geographic region and accompanied by useful job descriptions. Basic searches for salary by job title and geographic region are free, but fee-based "premium searches" also take into consideration your experience, performance, level of responsibility, and education as well as company size, location, and industry. Also features listings of jobs in the industry.

The *Wall Street Journal*'s Career Journal Site (www.careerjournal.com)

Provides industry insight, salary surveys, and career search advice to marketing job seekers. Review job openings by title, industry sector (including nonprofits, high-tech, service marketing, and CPG) or by region in the United States, Europe, or Asia. Use the "Salary and Hiring Info" tab to calculate pay for your target position by title and region. Although much of the content is geared toward managers and executives, advice, hiring trends, and data are available for recent college graduates, MBAs, and aspiring entrepreneurs.

Knowledge@Wharton (http://knowledge.wharton.upenn.edu)

This is an online resource for competitive intelligence in business and marketing, affiliated with the prestigious Wharton School of Business at the University of Pennsylvania. Articles and white papers cover current marketing and business trends, relevant business and academic research findings, interviews with industry leaders, conference and seminar reports, and book reviews. Select the marketing tab to access marketing resources, including articles and links to credible marketing resources. Subscriptions to free biweekly updates are available by clicking on the "sign up" tab. The site also offers a searchable database of articles and research abstracts, but one word of caution: This site can be slow to process requests.

WETFEET'S INSIDER GUIDE SERIES

JOB SEARCH GUIDES

Getting Your Ideal Internship

Job Hunting A to Z: Landing the Job You Want

Killer Consulting Resumes

Killer Investment Banking Resumes

Killer Resumes & Cover Letters

Negotiating Your Salary & Perks

Networking Works!

INTERVIEW GUIDES

Ace Your Case: Consulting Interviews

Ace Your Case II: 15 More Consulting Cases

Ace Your Case III: Practice Makes Perfect

Ace Your Case IV: The Latest & Greatest

Ace Your Case V: Return to the Case Interview

Ace Your Interview!

Beat the Street: Investment Banking Interviews

Beat the Street II: I-Banking Interview Practice Guide

CAREER & INDUSTRY GUIDES

Careers in Accounting

Careers in Advertising & Public Relations

Careers in Asset Management & Retail Brokerage

Careers in Biotech & Pharmaceuticals

Careers in Brand Management

Careers in Consumer Products

Careers in Entertainment & Sports

Careers in Human Resources

COMPANY GUIDES